The Wrights of Glenorchy

A Short History of

the Wright Family

1740 - 2010

Warren Dent
Seattle 2011

All rights reserved. No part of this book shall be reproduced or transmitted in any form or by any means, electronic, mechanical, magnetic, photographic including photocopying, recording or by any information storage and retrieval system, without prior written permission of the author. No patent liability is assumed with respect to the use of the information contained herein. Although every precaution has been taken in the preparation of this book, the author assumes no responsibility for errors or omissions. Neither is any liability assumed for damages resulting from the use of the information contained herein.

Copyright © 2011 by Warren Dent

ISBN 978-0-9834831-0-6

Printed in the United States of America

The Wrights of Glenorchy

A Short History of
the Wright Family
1740 - 2010

Warren Dent
Seattle 2011

The Wright Family Crest

In James Fairbairn's book "Fairbairn's Book of Crests of the Families of Great Britain and Ireland", p606, the crest for the Wright family is described as "a unicorn's head arg., erased gu., armed and maned or., charged on the neck with three spear-heads, one and two, also gu. *Mens conscia recti.*

Mens conscia recti is best translated as "your own inner knowledge that you have done right." It is incredibly appropriate for the Wrights of Glenorchy, as will be seen.

Dedicated to the modern day descendants of Stephen Amand Wright
and Lucy Elizabeth Tomkins who migrated from England in the
1840s and created a family which served the citizens
of Adelaide, South Australia and Glenorchy,
Tasmania in politics and agriculture,
generating a legacy of goodwill,
creativity, and industry
still recognized today.

Acknowledgments

Without the unselfish help of Gwenda Sheridan, landscape heritage expert,
and Scott Seymour, amateur historian and ardent musician,
this history would never have come to be told. As local
residents in the greater Hobart area they have
provided story and picture input impossible
to garner from afar. Interpretation of
their input remains the author's
however and they are free
from blame for mistakes,
omissions, and leaps
of faith.

Motivation

The link between author and the Wright family is tenuous to say the least. In the story that follows you will come to learn of Howard Edward Wright, grandson of Stephen Armand Wright. Howard married a lady from Sydney, Maude Florence Rogers. Maude was the daughter of the sister (Eliza Taylor) of the author's great great grandfather, Joseph Taylor, who came to Sydney in 1845/6.

In the author's genealogical lineage Maude is the one who 'strayed' most from the local family environs which were centered in Sydney and Maitland NSW. She gave up school teaching and married into this prominent Wright family.

On a visit to Tasmania the author found the ruins of the house where Howard lived as a teenager and young man. Being exposed to the history of the magnificent estate in which the house once stood in all its splendor captivated me and seemed deserving of greater publicity.

Here it is.

Author's note: This is a story. As far as possible it is based on fact. But as with all historical tales there are gaps in records and accounts where one can only guess what actually transpired. I have tried to minimize the interpretative 'leaps of faith' by including a vast array of footnotes involving newspaper clippings and other relevant records wherever possible. If the story helps others bring forth new related material that would be a wonderful result.

Finally, since I live in the US the book is written for both Australian and American audiences. Sometimes it deliberately uses American English spellings, at other times Australian English spellings. I saw no reason a priori to irritate only one group and not the other.

Wright Family Tree - Abbreviated

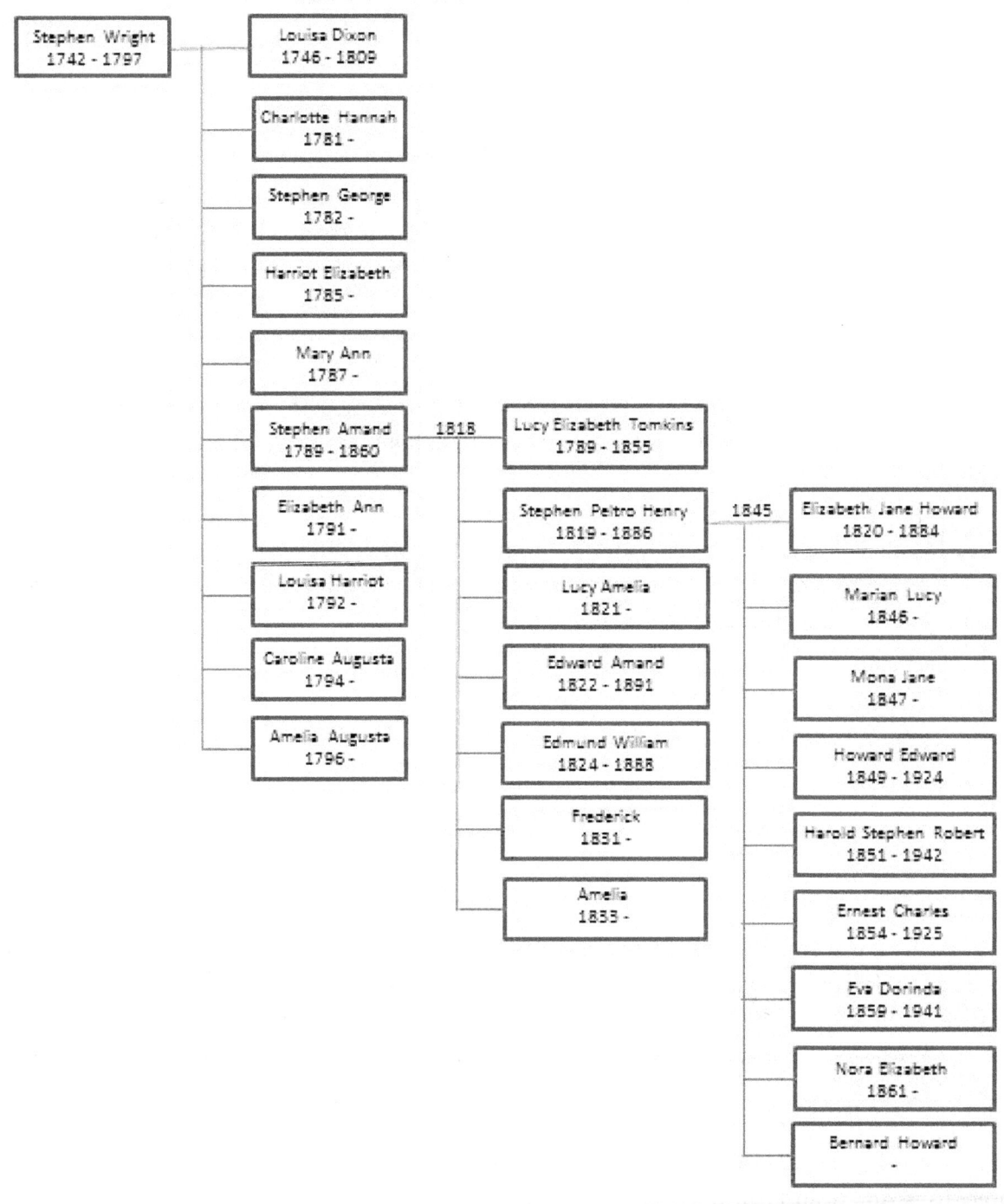

Contents

Chapter 1: From London, England to Adelaide, Australia..9

Chapter 2: The Grove..27

Chapter 3: Miscellany..41

Some Unanswered Questions 61

References..62

Permissions..63

Timeline...65

Footnotes Chapter 1...67

Footnotes Chapter 2...83

Footnotes Chapter 3...105

Chapter 1: From London, England to Adelaide, Australia

The evening was damp and cold, and the boisterous noise in the pub bounced off the walls, seemingly afraid to carry outside into the murky dark. Stephen Amand Wright swigged the last mouthful of ale from his tankard and gently put it down on the bench. "Then we are in agreement gentlemen – I'm glad we are of like mind. Thank you". Stephen's two friends, William Walker Gretton and John Wilson, also trustees of the estate of William's father John, finished their drinks, shook hands all round and hurried out through the front door of the White Swan public house in Mile End Rd., Stepney to take carriages home. It was early November 1842 and the three had agreed[1] to extend the lease on the public house and surrounding cottages to William Belton who had owned the buildings since Michaelmas 1814 per John Gretton's original lease agreement. As Barrister, William would have the agreement written up and they would all sign within the week.

The White Swan 556 Commercial Rd. Stepney

Stephen decided on one for the road before heading home to the West side of London, and reminisced over the wonderful companionship of his two friends. He remembered back to almost exactly 26 years before when on 28 Nov 1816 William had married his elder sister Mary Ann[2] at Stockwell Place in Surrey. What a grand occasion that was, although sad that their father Stephen and mother Louisa had not lived long enough to be present[3].

As for John - my gosh, John was now over 70 having been born 19 Aug 1770 in Edinburgh. He had known both Stephen and William's fathers and still had an incredibly sharp mind. John's 10 year younger brother Andrew was a famous landscape artist[4] and while closer to Stephen's age the two had never built a really strong friendship. Stephen had an important job as senior clerk in the Store Account Examiner's Office of the Ordnance Board at the Tower of London, and while a supporter of the Arts, enjoyed the responsibilities of the commercial world more.

All three men were well educated and highly intelligent. Compelling artistic ability and excellent business acumen had existed in all the families for years, and they were well known through the extended Lambeth area of London – Stockwell, Wandsworth, Clapham and Putney.

Stephen Amand Wright was the fifth of nine children born to Stephen Wright and Louisa Dixon[5]. He felt fortunate to have married Lucy Elizabeth Tomkins at St. George church, Hanover Square, twenty four years back on 14 Dec 1818[6]. Lucy was the eldest daughter of Lucy Jones and Peltro William Tomkins, an engraver and print publisher in New Bond St., the son of Susanna Callard and William Tomkins, a highly respected landscape artist[7]. Art ran in the Tomkins family and while Lucy also had creative talent she was a devoted mother to the six children she and Stephen had produced, four in early marriage years and two some years later.

Stephen's youngest sister Amelia Augusta, born in 1796, married Edward Le_Mesurier four years later in 1822[8]. Edward served as a lieutenant in the Royal Navy during the Napoleonic wars eventually settling in Genoa, Italy as a merchant. A daughter Amelia Louisa Vaux born 28 Dec 1823 married George Mussel Gretton in 1849[9], the third son of William Walter Gretton, thereby reuniting and reinforcing the ties between the Gretton and Wright families at another generation.

Over the years as Stephen's family grew they had changed locations to bigger houses, although always staying in the Lambeth area. Stephen had been born in 1789[10] in Stockwell and that was still a favourite haunt. The name Stokewell (first recorded in 1197) meant 'the well by the stump or wood' and came from the Old English stocc + wella. The manor of Stockwell was formed in the late 13th century, when King Edward I acquired the manor of South Lambeth and divided it into the two manors of Vauxhall and Stockwell.

Stockwell Grammar School 1830

In 1523 Sir John Leigh, Lord of the Manor, built the first Stockwell Chapel and in 1555 Queen Mary I granted Stockwell Manor to Viscount Montagu in recognition of his services during the rebellions of the Duke of Northumberland and Sir Thomas Wyatt. There was a Stockwell Wood until the 17th century. In 1683 part of the Manor was sold to John Howland, whose daughter Elizabeth married the Duke of Bedford. In 1767 the Church of St Andrew, Stockwell Green, was built on land given by the Duke of Bedford (the oldest church in Lambeth after St-Mary-at-Lambeth). And in 1802 the manor of Stockwell was sold at auction. Today, the oldest surviving buildings are St Andrew's Church, Stockwell Green c.1767 and Stockwell Congregational Church c.1798. The New Queen's Head in Stockwell Road retains its original late 18th century building[11].

Of unique historical interest, Stockwell was known as the center of tea smuggling in the 18th century. Tea used to be highly taxed by King Charles II, running at 119 per cent of the price of the goods. Fearful of the political intrigues that took place when people met in the beverage houses of London to drink tea and coffee, the government of the day decided a tax would prevent this. So in 1676, the humble cup of tea felt the heavy hand of the taxman. However, the people loved the drink. No tax would stop the sipping of a cup of tea. A black market in the leaf soon developed and bootlegging became a part of everyday trading.

Tea was so popular that big money could be made illegally, while pretending it was free trading. By the early 18th century the smuggling of tea into the country had become big business. Much of it came from Holland and was distributed from the south coast of England along a network of secret routes to the main market in the capital. The smuggling involved hundreds of people, usually organised in gangs. Ruthless in their pursuit of profit, all opposition to their smuggling was normally met with violence.

Naturally London was the biggest market. With its fashionable and wealthy society, it was the centre of the official tea trade. But many of the dealers were not above working with the smugglers, meeting with them secretly in Lambeth at the small village of Stockwell to strike deals. Here among the cottages lay a number of warehouses, owned or leased by the smuggling gangs, where tea was stored awaiting the dealers. The smugglers' route to Stockwell ran across Clapham Common, then a wild and unfriendly place and, on a Thursday in 1743, Custom and Excise officers were tipped off about a gang that would be crossing the common with horses loaded with tea. The armed revenue men lay in wait to ambush the gang. The smugglers - said to number

Swan Tavern 1860   Tea Smuggling Centre

more than twenty - arrived and stood their ground when confronted by the revenue men. Outnumbered, the officers retreated as the smugglers fired their guns and moved on with their contraband, cheering as they went. The smuggling of tea into London continued until the mid-18th century when the tax was dropped to popular acclaim. It established the 'cuppa' as Britain's national drink.

As the industrial age that started in the late 18th century gathered momentum in the early 1800s many Lambeth citizens were to lead very successful and rewarding lives, profiting from the demand for new industrial goods and appliances and the boom in real estate. But when the agrarian population revolted and fled massively to the cities in the 1840s, overcrowding and unemployment resulted. The outer suburbs of London deteriorated rapidly as crime became more prevalent, and the landed gentry felt dispossessed of their heritage and status. Artists went to Italy, and many businessmen headed for Australia.

The messages from the Antipodean colonies were improving monthly and to some it seemed there was more opportunity there than at home. Stephen's three eldest sons had already done well and he was inordinately proud of them so it was little surprise when Edward Amand, his second son, born in 1822[12], took off with a younger brother Frederick, born 1831[13],

The Port of Adelaide with Mt. Lofty 1845

for Adelaide in South Australia, where Edward set up business as a Land Agent.

The move was a very positive one and influenced Stephen's third son Edmund William, born 1824[14], who had recently returned from Bermuda, to follow his brothers' footsteps. He arrived in Port Adelaide May 1849 possibly on the Susannah of 514 tons, ex London 20th January or the Stebonheath, ex London 31st January and joined Edward in his agency and brokerage, but also immediately advertised his services as an architect[15] out of North Adelaide.

British Hotel Port Adelaide 1850

These were still very early and relatively primitive times, for Adelaide was well behind Sydney and other towns in its development. There were no Penal settlements so that labour for creating and maintaining Infrastructure was in low supply.

Indeed aborigines from the peaceful Kaurna tribe had small camps along the banks of the Torrens river and were far more prevalent than in other Australian towns.

But the climate was bearable, the soils rich and the location was bounded by the sea and pleasant rolling hills. For smart emigrant entrepreneurs the chance to become prosperous was very real and very attractive.

With clear sunshine, plenty of fresh water and space, glorious space, the town of Adelaide made London with its slums, crowds, crime, and dreary skies, a place to forget.

So now with three sons entrenched in Adelaide Stephen himself

Alexander Schramm   Aborigine gatherings, Adelaide 1850   NGA

considered a move to the colonies. He had been promoted to Master of Ordnance at the Tower of London[16] and was well off from his other dealings. His sons were delighted with the climate and the opportunities in their new land and wrote frequently to convince their father to join them.

Stephen pondered the alternatives. Stay with the companionship of his good friends and their families and his highly responsible and well respected job at the Tower, or join his growing antipodean family in a sunny land where poverty and disillusionment were minimal and investment opportunity abounded. Even now in 1849 he was still a young sixty years old. But retirement would be called for this year. Perhaps that was appropriate as he walked less and used carriages quite a bit more than he did just five years ago. Beyond that, certainly the increasing pollution and social plight of Lambeth was more distressing and depressing each year. His two daughters still depended on him, although his first son was totally self-sufficient.

He gathered his family together in late Fall and after prolonged discussion decided a move to Australia would be good for all of them. Feelings of excitement, trepidation, fear and elation vied for presence over the next few months as plans solidified and were implemented. A lot would be left for the eldest son Stephen Peltro Henry born in 1819[17] and now 30 years old to manage after the others had gone, but he was well and truly up to the task with an innate sense of responsibility and family obligation. He had married Elizabeth Jane Howard in 1845 and they already had 3 fine children, the youngest, Howard, being born just a few days earlier[18].

And thus on the 16th January 1850, Stephen took his wife Lucy, his two daughters, Lucy Amelia born 22 Mar 1821[19], and Amelia born in 1833[20], to the docks in London and boarded the Fatima, a brand new barque of 500 tons, destined to sail on the morrow for Plymouth and thence to Adelaide[21].

The hustle and bustle around the Fatima was at the frantic level as the last provisions and animals were swung on board and as cabin passengers were helped up the gangways with all their belongings, most of which would be stored in the hold. Some of the 'government passengers' or 'emigrants' travelling under the United Kingdom assisted passage schemes, which had started just three years earlier, were also boarding, certainly with far less belongings. These travellers, in steerage apartments, were divided into three groups – families, single men, and single women and children. On inquiring of Master Ray, the Captain, Stephen learned that he anticipated 165 in families. 33 single men, 23 single women and 3 children along with 15 in the cabins for a total complement of 239 passengers.

Fine example of a barque early 1800s

Some of course, especially those from Ireland and the Cornwall area, were to be picked up in Plymouth. Stephen also learned that the vast majority of males were labourers, with only a few having a trade- including a butcher, carpenter, blacksmith, shepherd, wheelwright, bricklayer and saddler. Most of the single women were servants and the vast majority of all passengers were under thirty years old. He and his wife would be among the eldest on board. After quickly organizing the cabin allotted to him and his wife he sought out and introduced himself to the Surgeon on board – Dr. John Wilkins. Other cabin passengers would be joining at Plymouth he learned.

And of course when the morrow eventually came the ship was not yet ready to sail with the late arrival of some goods and a number of lagging emigrants. It was late afternoon before getting underway on Thursday January 17th.

Finally the great adventure had begun. As the enormous rope lines were freed from the oversized cleats and sailors manoeuvered the massive ship slowly away from the wharf Stephen offered a silent prayer that his intuition would be proven justified and that the promised land would fulfill his dreams for all his family.

The run down the Thames past Gravesend where they anchored overnight was relatively uneventful but heading east into the windswept North Sea and then south past Ramsgate and southwest to Dungeness, the exuberance on board rapidly disappeared as the rolling and pitching of the vessel made the 'land-lubbers' sea-

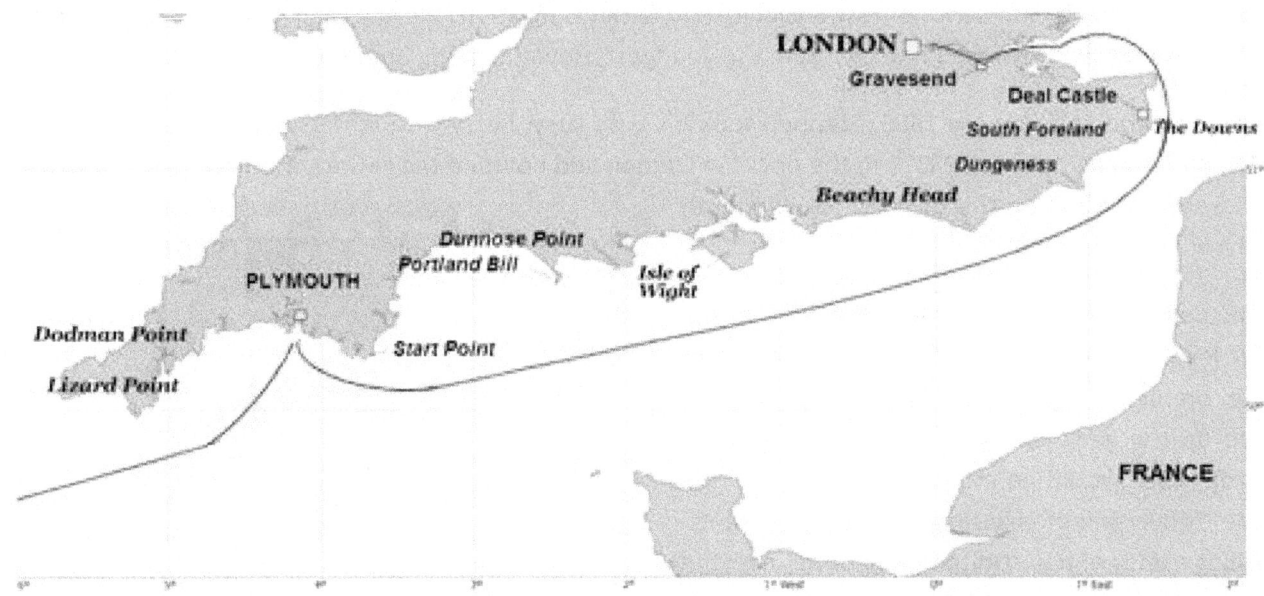

sick. South of Brighton a fearsome gale arose and little progress was made over several days as they were drenched by rain and forced by winds in too southerly a direction, taking the ship way off course - seemingly closer to France than the mother country. Eventually of course the rain ceased and the winds abated, with no damage to the masts, booms or rigging, but some tearing of sails which were quickly mended over the next two days as the sun broke through the clouds.

For most on board this was in fact their first trip on a sailing vessel and the experience to date was far worse than what they had been led to believe. Many wondered whether the Fatima would ever make Plymouth, let alone Adelaide on the other side of the world. Despite the Surgeon's and Captain's reassurances some of the emigrants were frightened nearly out of their minds and their wailing continued night and day until the ship finally limped into the Sound off Plymouth on Monday February 4th. Many of these 'invalids' as the crew termed them wanted to leave ship but with government-paid passages, and with their abodes now abandoned, there was really no such option.

A calm day on Tuesday allowed more provisioning at the docks and the taking on board of the Clark family – Mr. & Mrs. and 8 children for the cabins, as well as many more emigrants and, also for the cabins, a well-educated young teenager Henry Hobhouse Turton, who immediately asked to be called Harry by all. The ship was then towed to the Catwater in the East where some minor repairs were carried out.

The following day the ship was towed back out to the Sound where everyone rested up. But on the Friday and Saturday a heavy rainstorm passed through and Lucy senior and Miss Lucy were decidedly unwell. They brightened that evening as the Northern lights flashed in the skies. Sunday was fine but on Monday and Tuesday it rained again. Finally on Wednesday 13th February the ship made ready to leave. Two daughters from the Browne family, friends of the Wrights, came on board to wish them well, and just before noon the Captain weighed anchor and the Fatima headed south and west into the Atlantic before a northwest wind.

The next two days found most of the new emigrants seasick and the Surgeon was obliged to introduce an airsail into the 'tween decks. It had the effect of bringing fresh air into the emigrant apartments, which helped enormously. One woman put her arm out of joint, but the Surgeon set it right in short order. All the Wrights were so ill that none ventured on deck Thursday but Stephen and Miss Lucy couldn't resist checking the Lizard lights late Friday afternoon – signaling the last sight of the English mainland.

After two days of reasonable sailing, on Monday Feb 18th towards 2 o'clock a Pilot boat from the Scilly Isles came alongside, and promised to report the Fatima 'all well'; the Captain threw the sailors a piece of pork and beef; they took two letters for Mr. Clark, which were wrapped in a piece of oilskin and thrown over with the meat. In the evening towards 6 o'clock the Scilly lighthouse became visible; it burned a revolving light, which was only visible for a few seconds in every minute.

On board an emigrant ship on the long voyage to Australia. (M.W. Ridley)

And so with England now behind them and the vast Atlantic ahead the passengers started to settle into an everyday routine. By Friday Feb 22nd the boat was 400 miles off Plymouth at Latitude 45° 3' North, Longitude 11° 3' West running rather slowly against contrary winds. Each evening the Captain posted the ship's position with a reckoning on the distance travelled in the previous 24 hours. By now the water had changed colour and was beautifully transparent, and jellyfish abounded .

A sad event occurred on Sunday Feb 24th when before dawn ten year old Catherine Stone suddenly died from reasons unknown. The funeral was performed later that morning at about 9:30. Her mattress and pillow were first thrown overboard; then the body was carried up on deck, where the burial service was read by the

Surgeon; the Union Jack was hoisted, and the flag was also laid over the body. Three other children remained in the family and the mother and father were distraught.

Two days later the weather was fine and a northwest wind had picked up enabling a speed of some 7 knots with 170 miles covered in 24 hours. In the evening of Thursday Feb 28 a good deal of phosphoric light was evident in the water. It was smoother than the day before, when the spray occasionally dashed over the bulwarks, onto the main deck and gave the emigrants a washing.

The ship proceeded south heading slightly towards the African coastline and on Mar 3rd the Desertas Islands and Madeira came into view. Great quantities of porpoises surrounded the ship; they came in herds at intervals; some seemed to be racing, and jumped over 20 feet out of the water together. Seeing Faro, Palma and Ferro islands over the next couple of days gave everyone cheer. The peaks of Tenerife were clearly visible even though ninety miles distant. By now the invalids seemed better and the four Wrights and most of the Clarks were often out walking the decks with the rest of the passengers.

By March 7 the ship was in the tropics, the water had resumed more of its green colour, most probably from the nearness to the African coast. Anticipating the heat ahead, the Surgeon had ordered the emigrants to have all their children's hair cut; but upon examination 24 were found not cut at all. The Doctor then told these that if it was not done, that he should take doing so into his own hands. That morning at 9 o'clock there was only one rebellious emigrant, who besides refusing to cut his little girl's hair, was insolent to the Doctor, who then put hand cuffs on him. As he was taking the child to cut her hair the father still tried to prevent him. At this point however the Captain interceded, and knocked the father down. This brought all the emigrants up from below, and there was a terrible scene of crying, abusing, etcetera. The emigrants were very angry at the Captain, who had however provided himself with a pistol. There were three women in particular who argued and screeched vociferously. In about an hour's time though everything had become quiet. During the disturbance the Doctor had cut the child's hair, the man was still in irons, and seemed still angry, as he had threatened to murder Mr. Browne, another of the emigrants. For this he would be kept a prisoner until he promised to keep the peace, and begged the Doctor's pardon. Miss Wright fainted during the afternoon as she had not been very well all morning during the altercation.

Before breakfast the next morning a large whale about 40' long was seen not far from the ship, and all those on deck could follow his track quite well for some distance. Grampusses (dolphins) and flying fish appeared during the afternoon along with Portuguese men of war, and while the weather was pleasant enough there was an unusual spate of accidents in a short period. A little boy fell down the main hatchway, a spar fell on a woman's wrist, and another woman went into a fit. The Surgeon was busy. Mrs. Clark kindly talked to the prisoner and his wife, persuading the man to apologise to the Doctor for his misconduct, and promising to keep the peace during the rest of the voyage. The Doctor gladly released him, and he became quite useful to the sailors afterwards.

On Monday the 11th the emigrants brought their trunks up, and consequently the deck was in great confusion. There was one Irish woman, who had been so furious with her tongue two days previously, saying she had more silk dresses etc than all the Cabin passengers put together. On inspection however only three fine bonnets, and the same number of caps were discovered. More unfathomable accidents occurred - the Ship's

Carpenter, while chopping a piece of wood, cut one of his toes all but off; in fact it was only hanging on by a piece of skin, and two others he cut to the bone.

By Thursday Mar 14 the ship was at Latitude 6° 24' N. Longitude 20° 46' W., well off the African coast and heading for the equator. It was a very hot day; the thermometer on deck was at 81 ½° and in the cabin at 81°. The ship had made 136 miles in the 24 hours, and during the day had traveled at about 5 knots. At 11 am an immense number of Porpoises came by, probably more than 200; they came jumping out of the water, so that they were able to be seen for some distance. One turned a double somersault in the air, and then fell clumsily back into the water. In the afternoon some Grampusses were seen about the ship. One of Mrs. Clark's sons had put out a line to catch the dolphins, but on pulling up his line he found the hook broken right in half. At 6pm some very dark clouds appeared, and it began to rain. At midnight, after all the ladies had retired, the Doctor, Harry, and Mr. Clark junior took a bath, by throwing buckets of water over each other, which was very refreshing; the water was very warm, and the phosphoric light which remained on their bodies rendered it very curious.

Now, due to perverse winds, progress slowed and in some cases reversed so that it was not until Thursday Mar 21st that the Fatima finally crossed the equator. The heat brought on several fits among the emigrants and on the 24th an alarming incident occurred in which a fire rushed out of the Emigrants Galley, which if water had not been immediately procured would have caught on the sails which were very near. The emigrants of course were making all the noise they could, which together with the fright had the effect of once again setting the invalids into fits immediately. The fire was caused by one of the emigrants putting some suet on the stove, which running down into the fire made it blaze up in this alarming manner.

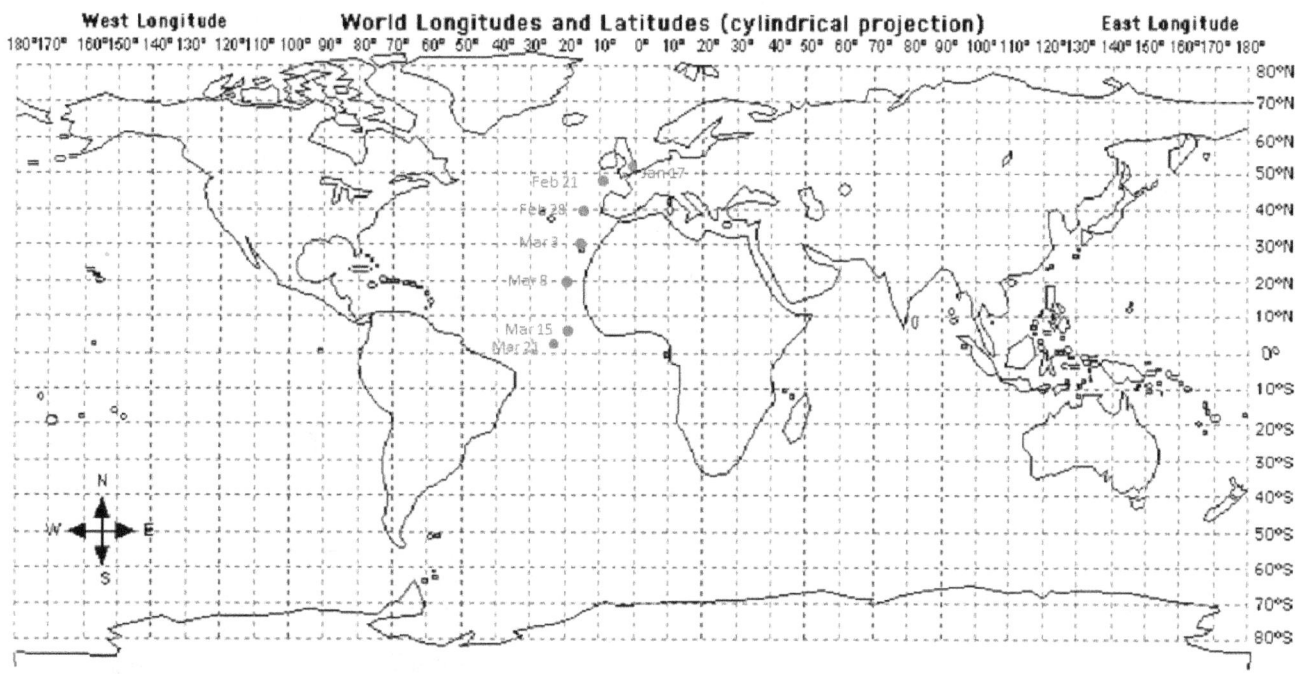

The route of the Fatima – London Jan 17 to Mar 21 1850

On the morning of Mar 27 a Porpoise was captured by the sailors, and was immediately hauled up under the bough, where he was left until he was dead. He was then safely paraded on the main deck for general inspection, and was then cut up. In the afternoon a portion was cooked, and distributed amongst the emigrants and sailors; those in the cabins heard that it ate very much like beef. He was about 6 feet in length, and from what the sailors said contained a good deal of oil. The sunset was one of the most beautiful seen on the trip; the dark vermilion intermixed with the dark blue clouds rendered it very rich, and at the same time the moon was slowly appearing above the horizon, which added still more to the beauty of the scene. At about midnight a squall passed over, bringing with it a smart breeze, which continued during the night.

Mar 27th was a pleasant day, with a fine breeze, which carried the ship along at 8 knots. The log showed 163 miles in the 24 hours. There was already a very perceptible difference in the temperature. The day before a schooner had been seen, steering more to the westward, evidently bound to South America.

A fine breeze (of eight knots) during the night of Friday Mar 29 enabled the Fatima to make the longest run since leaving Plymouth, namely 183 miles. The temperature was now much more agreeable to all, being about 80° on deck. Mr. Thornton, the Second Mate had saved the Porpoise's head, and young Harry went with him on the forecastle, where it was hanging. For fun, as apparently was the custom, Harry was seized quite unexpectedly by the sailors, who chaulked his shoes, and kept him prisoner until he promised to pay a fine, being a bottle of Grog. The invalids were still having fits, but received several boxes on the ear and face from the Surgeon hoping to calm them down – an unusual approach indeed, but apparently reserved for when nothing else worked.

On March 30th another accident occurred. About 2 in the afternoon, while all were busily occupied on deck, there was a sudden cry of 'man overboard'. The helm was immediately put down, the ship wore round, life buoys were thrown over, and the Jolly boat, which was in the midst of being painted, was lowered. In the meantime many had been watching the sailor, who fortunately was a very good swimmer, raising himself above water as much as possible so as to be seen. On seeing the boat he immediately swam for it, and before ½ an hour had expired, he was safely landed on the sailors' 'Terra Firma'. He seemed very little exhausted, because in another 5 minutes he was taking his place at the ropes with the other sailors. The accident was occasioned by a piece of spun yarn breaking to which he was holding on to while working on the fore-rigging. In the fall he knocked his head against some chains which rendered him insensible for a minute or two in the water. This was not the only misfortune which occurred, for in the lowering of the boat, one of the sailors caught his thumb between the ship and the boat. He was obliged to have his nail taken off, which is a very painful operation. The emigrants as usual were all confusion, crying, screaming, and fits were the order of the day. When the poor sailor reached the boat there was a general hurrahing.

Worse, the very next day two small children died of infantile fever. One was named Elizabeth, and happened to be the five year old sister of the little girl who had died earlier. The other was named Grace Bickerton, whose parents William and Margaret were aged 24 and 23 with a remaining five year old

Sea Burial

daughter, named Margaret after her mother. There was very little one could do to comfort the four grieving parents but a pall was cast across the ship with such sadness in the air.

With the Southeast Trades now gone speed dropped markedly and there were days when the ship was almost becalmed. Saturday April 5th seemed to be a turning point, almost literally. At Latitude 29° 58' S. and Longitude 30° 52' W. a nice westerly breeze picked up heading the ship back towards the southern African coast. Heavy squalls turned into a gale over the next several days making meals impossible affairs as plates tipped over and soup spilt into laps, causing Sunday services to be abandoned, and generally wreaking havoc for all with drenched clothes from spray over the poop, caps lost to the wind, and eyes 'washed' with salt water.

Leaving the tropics behind the weather improved again. A young baby, now 3 weeks old was brought on deck for the first time and seemed to enjoy the fresh air and sunshine. And now giant albatrosses with wing spans up to thirteen feet came flying in, circling the ship out of curiosity. The ship's speed reached upward of ten knots in the following days and on April 17th contact was made with another barque, the Wugear, bound for Calcutta and 69 days out, a few days more than the Fatima's journey ex Plymouth. Stephen Wright had fallen and hurt himself severely during the recent gale but was now up and about which was good to see as the Wrights were a popular family on board – especially the two daughters - Miss Lucy who was 29 and Miss Amelia 17.

Five days later, now East of Greenwich mean time, as the temperature was becoming cooler, a large number of Albatrosses came by. Lines with hooks and bait flying from the masts intrigued the birds and two were caught, one by young Mr. Turton, who wanted it stuffed and preserved. It turned out that there was an avid naturist artist on board in one of the Clark daughters who took great delight in sketching and sometimes

painting both fish and birds that appeared on the ship, as well as the sailors executing their duties.

Coming nearer to the Cape of Good Hope more birds of varied species started to appear. Ships on the route to Australia no longer felt it necessary to always stop in Capetown and the Fatima was no exception. On April 28th a number of passengers wrote letters and sealed them in a bottle tossed overboard wondering if anyone would ever find same and respond. An emigrant who also happened to be a Mrs. Jane Wright gave birth to a young boy. She had suffered miserably through the hot tropics but now was thoroughly relieved.

May 1st found the Fatima due south of the Cape well on an easterly course into the Indian Ocean and with Australia dead ahead. Winds were only fair during the first week of May but then picked up with squalls and heavy seas but the 24 hours ending at 10pm on May 9th added 218 miles to the distance travelled – a record since leaving Plymouth. On the 13th the emigrants once again brought their luggage on deck and reorganized. The 'squaw 'seemed happier than ever pawing through her seemingly endless supply of silk dresses and fine shawls. When she came to the bottom of the box, she worked to repack what others felt was totally useless finery. No matter, each emigrant had their little treasures and reminders of home.

By May 16th the Fatima came upon the islands of St. Paul and Amsterdam. The two islands are located at 37° 50' S. and 77° 35' E., and are amongst the most isolated in the world. They are more than 3,000 km from any continent, approximately halfway between South Africa and Australia. Both are volcanic, rising from the fault separating the Indian Ocean from the Antarctic Ocean. Amsterdam is broadly oval in shape, measuring eight km wide by six km across, with a maximum altitude of 881 m. The two islands lie on a narrow ridge which falls to great depths. Of very recent formation, Amsterdam is a relatively simple volcano made up of deposits of lava and basaltic slag from the successive eruptions of the various craters on the island. There are more than ten different craters. The principal craters, believed to have created the island, are those of Mont de la Dive (867m) and La Grande Marmite (730m). Lava flows radiate outwards from these craters, forming low cliffs where they meet the sea. One of many hot springs is 200° hot. Martin de Viviès base is the only inhabited place on Amsterdam. It has about 30 inhabitants, including administrative staff, a doctor, technical personnel (power station, plumbing, joinery, kitchen, store, station and telecomms) and scientists (studying the weather, ornithology, physicochemistry of the atmosphere and geomagnetism). To the passengers on the Fatima, even though the mountainous rocks were stark, after two months at sea with no sight of land they were deemed incredibly 'picturesque'.

Squalls from the north through May 20, while unpleasant, helped drive the ship east at a good rate. On May 21st another one of those unexplainable incidents occurred. Mr. Wright and Harry found a young man sitting in a tub, which the Carpenter had converted into a chair to let the ladies down at the end of the voyage, on the deck and looking very ill. Upon enquiry it seems he had been formerly engaged to a Miss White, an emigrant on board, and whilst he was laid up with a bad leg, which he had cut with an adze, she re-engaged herself to another of the single men. He took this so much to heart that it obviously affected his mental health, and he was delirious all the previous day, and now hardly knew what he was doing.

Six days later the Captain, crew and passengers rejoiced somewhat in considering themselves under the lee of the Australian coast, having passed Cape Leeuwin within the previous twenty four hours. But driven southward shortly thereafter a course correction had to be made and on May 30th inattention on the part of some of the sailors caused the main topgallant yard to be broken, for which the boys all received a ropes ending, as a punishment for their carelessness.

The whole first week of June brought soft or adverse winds yielding slow speeds and inevitable course adjustments. It was as if Adelaide wasn't sure whether it wanted the Fatima to arrive or not. Saturday June 8 brought great excitement with the shout of "Land-Ho" reverberating around the ship.

On June 10th early in the morning Kangaroo Island became imperfectly visible through a thick drizzling rain. In the afternoon the land became much plainer and a small cutter passed very near. Everyone expected to see the Lightship about 6 o'clock, but it being very hazy, and the wind changing a little the ship was not able to make it, and accordingly tacked at that hour. After tea some lights were seen, one of which was concluded to be the Lightship, the others ships. On the strength of this observation the ship anchored at about 8 o'clock. At 10pm there was a heavy squall which made the Captain very uneasy, and he ordered the other anchor to be made ready in case one was insufficient to hold the ship.

But hold it did and on Tuesday the 11th of June the anchor was weighed at 10am when the pilot came on board and the ship moved closer to the Lightship where it awaited a steam tug to guide it up the Torrens river to the docks.

Any new ship arrival was an exciting event for many residents anticipating supplies and possible relatives. The Fatima's arrival was no exception and as the four members of the Wright family crowded the ship's rail a boat came by with Stephen's three sons – Edmund, Edward and Frederick. At first neither group recognized the other, but at last the three men climbed on board and the happiest of reunions with tears and laughter took place. Stephen, his wife Lucy, and daughters Miss Lucy and Miss Amelia were reunited with loving sons and brothers after an inordinately long period of over 140 days at sea. No doubt it took several days before their sea legs fully acclimatised to real 'terra firma' once again[22].

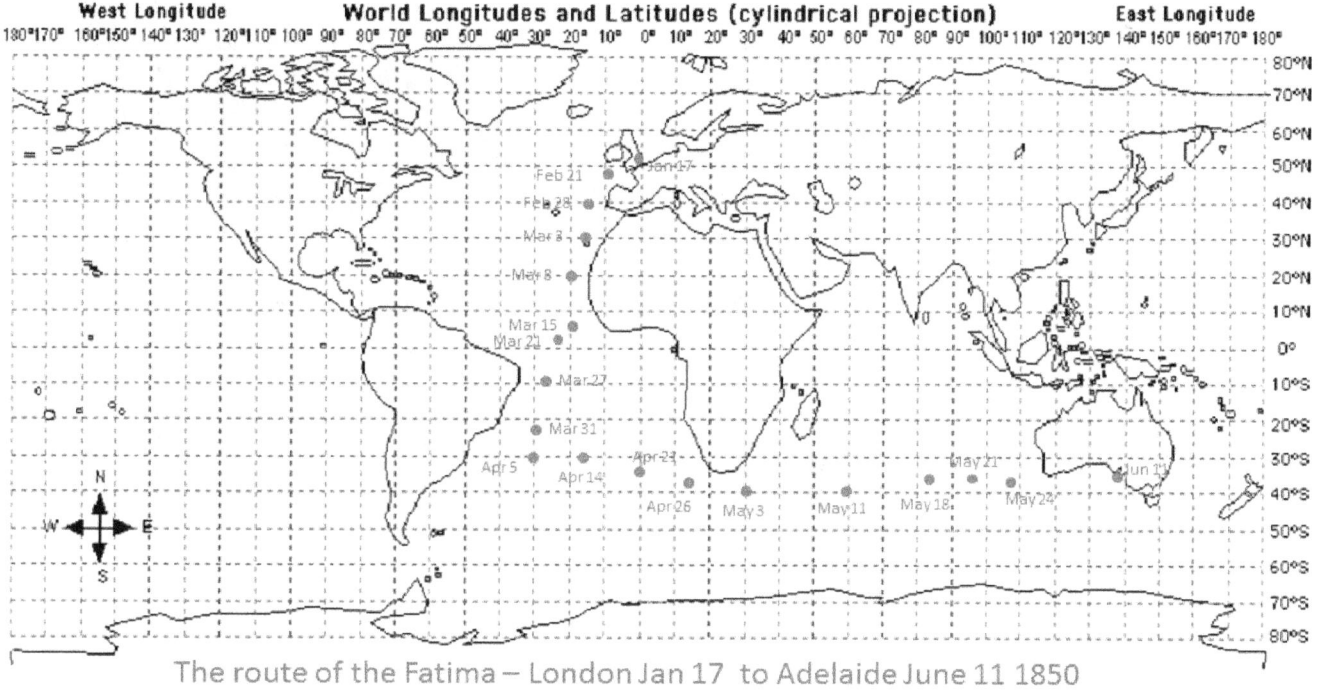

The route of the Fatima – London Jan 17 to Adelaide June 11 1850

The next important task confronting the new family arrivals was to learn about their new city and its offerings. Adelaide had a strong English flavour with a large population of free settlers and assisted emigrants so that wherever possible residents recreated their British heritage in juxtaposition with their new environment.

The city clearly appealed to Stephen and Lucy from the outset and with the help of their architect son Edmund they designed a new home in the suburb of West Torrens. Built in 1851, in deference to the beautiful flora of the city's surrounding hills, they named their new abode "The Gums"[23].

Back in England the remaining son Stephen Peltro Henry had followed in his father's footsteps and was now a clerk in the Ordnance Department at the Tower and living in High Street, Putney. Just as "The Gums" was finished being built a letter arrived indicating that Stephen's wife Elizabeth had delivered a son Harold Stephen Robert on 21 Sep 1851. That made 2 boys and two girls. Stephen was managing all the local affairs and his family was doing well.

Earlier in June, Edmund took over the practice of architect Henry Stuckey, who had died the previous May. A little over a year later, on 26 October 1852, he married Agnes Rippingville, Stuckey's widow[24]. He bought and extended the cottage which Stuckey had been renting at 26 Palmer Place, North Adelaide.

Less than a year later on 19th Mar 1853 brother Edward, now living in Lockleys, married Lucy Ann Windsor in Hobart[25]. The Win(d)sor family could trace their roots back to Modbury, Devon in England to a James Winsor born in 1597[26]. Lucy was the fourth of ten children, all but the last being born in England, but all migrating to Hobart by 1840. She and Edward returned from Hobart to North Adelaide to raise a family.

And so the Wright family expanded. Back in Putney Stephen Peltro and Elizabeth had another son, Ernest Charles, in 1854. And now Stephen himself was thinking of coming to Adelaide and joining his brothers and sisters and parents who loved it there.

In 1855 he made the big decision and hastened to Adelaide[27], driven in part by the news that his mother was not well. He arrived in time for her to meet her latest grandson, but unfortunately she succumbed shortly thereafter on 12 Sep and was buried in the beautiful and select pioneer portion of the cemetery at Mitcham[28].

Entrance Mitcham Anglican Cemetery

Before she died however she was able to meet Lucy Amelia's beau, Peter Prankerd, a rich English gentleman who had travelled extensively in the South Pacific and had prospered through smart investments in copper mines. He and Lucy were married a year later in Christ Church, North Adelaide on 8 Mar 1856[29].

Christ Church, North Adelaide ca. 1870

Now the whole family lived in the immediate surrounds of Adelaide, helping each other with social and business connections, thereby enabling all the members to prosper and enjoy their new home so many miles away from England.

Stephen and Lucy's prayers were fulfilled.

More grandchildren continued to arrive as Edward and Lucy's first child Blanche was born 22 Sep 1857. In 1858, the prominence of the Wrights became highly public, for in recognition of his business acumen and civic pride and contributions, Stephen Peltro Henry Wright was elected Mayor of Glenelg[30], no mean achievement having arrived in the community just three years earlier.

Stephen Peltro Henry Wright
1858

Aside from helping the citizens of Glenelg through his new office Stephen inspired his brother Edmund to also enter the political scene. In 1859 Edmund became Mayor of Adelaide, but resigned eleven months later, for which he was fined £10[31]. The previous year he had won a competition to design a new town hall but the council could not raise the money to build it. Also in 1859 Stephen and Elizabeth brought Eva Dorinda into the world and Edward and Lucy brought Edith Amelia along.

Once again the prominence of the family was well recognized in invitations to attend the Ball at Government House in honour of Her Majesty's birthday May 19 1859. It was a grand occasion well covered in the newspaper of the day[32].

In January of 1860 Frederick married Frances Jane O'Halloran, 3rd of 4 children born to Thomas Shuldham O'Halloran and Jane Waring, originally from Devon, England. Sadly however, in March of 1860 the Wright family patriarch Stephen Amand died while on a trip to Paris. His remains were returned to Adelaide and he was buried alongside his wife Lucy at the Michigan Anglican Cemetery[33].

The rest of the 1860s saw widespread expansion of the remaining family. Edmund and Agnes added three children alongside Agnes' daughter from her previous marriage. In 1861 babies were born to Frederick and Frances, Edward and Lucy, Stephen and Elizabeth, and Lucy and Peter. 1862 and 1863 saw two more births to Frederick and Frances, with Lucy and Peter contributing again in 1864, and Stephen and Elizabeth adding two more by 1864.

In 1865 winds of change started to arrive and the heat of summers made family members look to alternative places to live. In November of that year Stephen resigned as Mayor of Glenelg and put his enormous house up for rent[34]. His brother Edward was the real estate agent handling the arrangements.

Finally in the unpleasant heat of middle summer, on Thursday January 18 1866, Stephen, Lucy and the children boarded the Coorong, a steamer of 390 tons, bound for Melbourne. After a short stay there the family continued to Hobart on the Derwent of 350 tons.

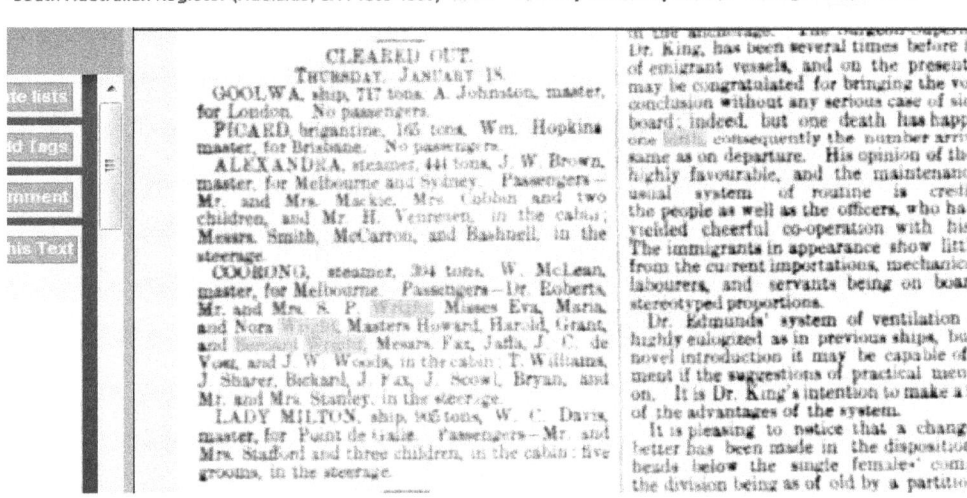

Son "Grant" is probably a mistake and should be Ernest. Also daughter Mona is missing from this list

Coorong 1862 - 1911

The Coorong was an iron steamship powered by 2 cylinders producing 70 horsepower. It was originally built in Glasgow for an investor in Adelaide but changed ownership many times up to 1911 when she was hulked in Sydney.

The Derwent built in 1864 was a sister ship to the 1862 built propeller-driven steamship Tasmania plying the Melbourne - Hobart route. The two were stars of the Tasmanian Steam Navigation (TSN) company welcomed especially by merchants in Hobart and the Tasmanian countryside[35].

The Derwent was bigger than the Cooroong and more powerful, generating 120 horsepower. In 1879 she was bought by the Melbourne Steamship Company. For a while she ran between Sydney and northern Queensland before being brought back on Victorian coastal routes. Eventually in 1925 she was hulked in northern Queensland

Derwent 1864 - 1915

The boats carried a limited number of passengers and were primarily used to transport freight between ports. For Tasmania sea transport was vitally important. On the mainland rail carriage eventually overtook ship traffic for freight transportation.

And so a new life began for the Stephen Peltro Henry Wright family. Tasmania, and the Hobart area in particular, offered a much cooler climate than the Adelaide suburbs. In fact Tasmania was often publicised as a better place for one's health than elsewhere. Of course there was an extensive penal colony at Port Arthur and more convicts in the town and countryside than in Adelaide. But also there was a lot of fertile ground along the Derwent river for crops and livestock. And constant streams of fresh water flowed from the gullies of Mt. Wellington, which dominated the Hobart skyline.

Here then were boundless business opportunities attracting the politically astute and highly creative Wrights that added to the other benefits of climate and better health offered in this new location. Stephen bought a house first in Davey St., Hobart, then later moved north of Hobart to O'Brien's Bridge, which later became part of the town of Glenorchy where he soon became a member of the town council.

In 1868 he bought what was known as "The Grove Estate", 46 acres of land bounded on the East by Humphrey's rivulet and in the North by the Derwent[36]. Little did he know at the time how incredibly influential he and The Grove and his family would become, not only in the development of the surrounding town, but also in the world agricultural commerce scene and the High Society of Hobart.

Stephen, a natural leader with foresight and ingenuity, was literally about to bring significant changes to the world he and millions of others currently knew.

Author's note: The footnotes to this chapter entail an enormous richness of research into family histories. Much more detail could have been provided but would have detracted from the story aspect above. Significant prominent English families surrounded the Wrights wherever they alighted – in Surrey, in Adelaide, and (to be shown) Glenorchy and Hobart. Their social standing had them hobnobbing with the rich, famous and influential. These relationships themselves would make another intriguing story, as would the lineage of many of the families. Where possible that lineage has in fact been captured in a separate database, available upon request. In some instances, despite intensive research, some details remain incomplete – eg. birthdates of Stephen's son Bernard. Possible death dates have not always been sought, and as is the case with old records, some inconsistencies arise - such as the numbers and names of Stephen's children on ships between Adelaide and Melbourne and Melbourne and Hobart.

And as with all such stories there will always remain unanswered questions. The biggest in my mind is why the first Wrights ever sought to go to Adelaide. Were there friends or contacts there who sent letters home telling of the charm of the city, the little English community with no convicts, and the good living possible? Or were family fortunes being challenged back in Lambeth as the economy deteriorated, making Australia, the new land of opportunity, simply seem very attractive in its own right? Did members of other well-known families, friends of the Wrights, migrate later? It seems highly possible but has not been explored.

As will be further evidenced, the business skills the Wrights developed were transferable into varied occupations, seemingly all the more remarkable for the times. These were indeed extraordinary people. Unlike those who first created paths through the bush, cleared the land, and first established primitive settlements. But pioneers in their own right, who with imagination and hard work built businesses based on the resources at hand, and who unselfishly helped create communities and provided employment for hundreds of others. In so doing they not only benefitted their fellow citizens, but championed principles and qualities that became the foundation of many values the young country adopted in its historical growth.

Their tale continues…..

Chapter 2: The Grove

The first land grants to settlers anxious to live in the area north of Hobart on the western bank of the Derwent were made in 1804. At that time government officials and free settlers established homes on the banks of what became known as the New Town Rivulet which brought water off the slopes of Mt. Wellington down to the river. They cleared the land and established crops and pastures and became suppliers of grain and meat to the commissariat in Hobart. By 1816 an extensive district running north from the New Town Rivulet was well known for its agricultural products. Another set of farms was grouped along Humphrey's Rivulet forming a settlement called O'Brien's Bridge. The only commercial buildings by 1820 included an Inn and a Water Mill. Humphrey's Rivulet forked as it neared the river and the land between was known as the Montrose Farm. For a while it was owned by Robert Littlejohn who died in 1819 with the farm subsequently being put up for sale. An 1820 map of Glenorchy still labels the farm with the name Littlejohn[1].

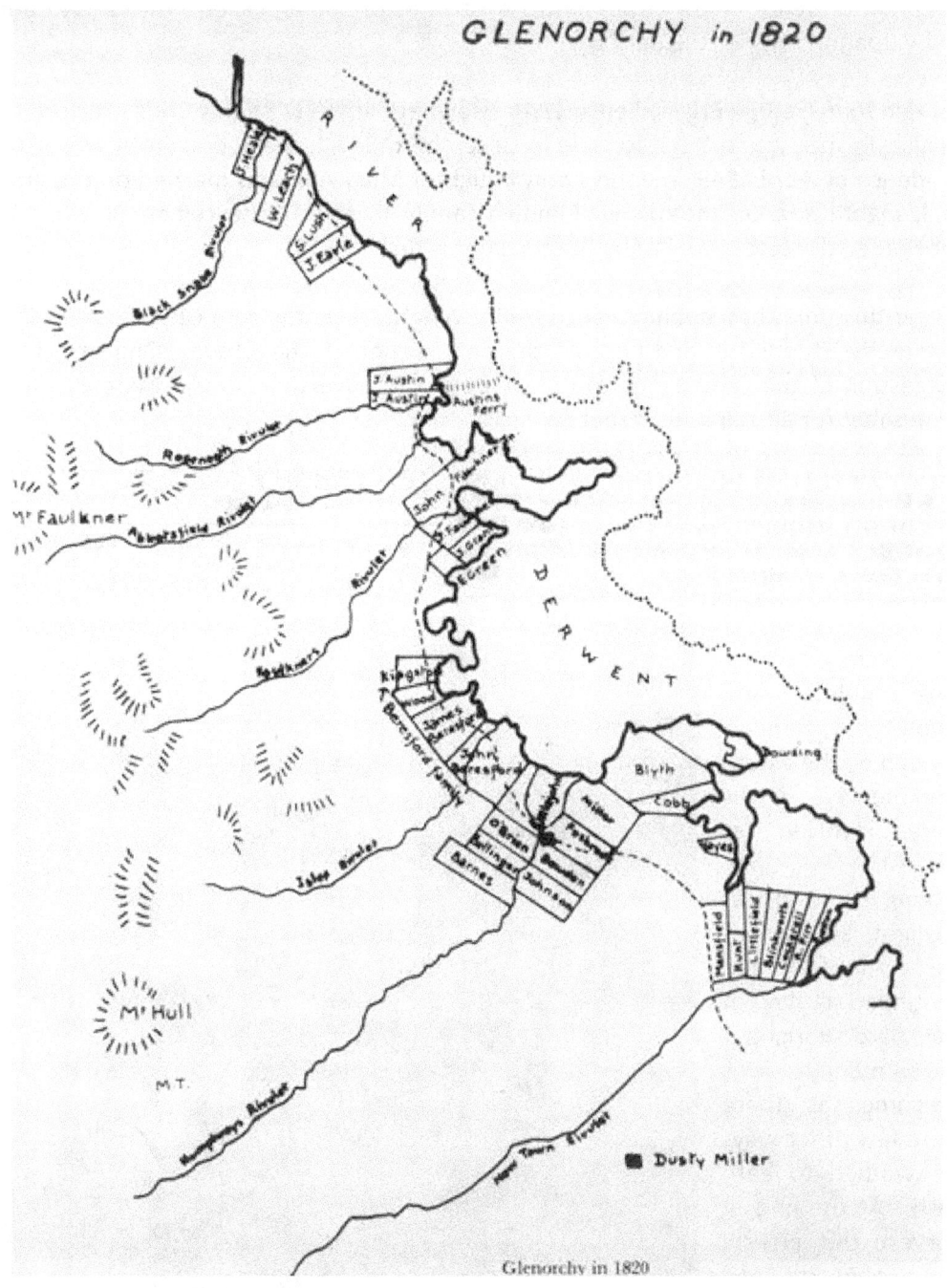

Glenorchy in 1820

The farm sat on over 100 acres with several in cultivation and held large stands of timber. There was a neat little weather-boarded cottage, shingled and glazed, with a garden already stocked with a variety of fruit trees[2].

It's not clear who bought the farm subsequently, but by 1832 it was owned by a Mr. Stocker – most likely the butcher in Collins and later Elizabeth Sts. in Hobart Town who owned extensive fattening yards and slaughtering facilities. By then the farm had 30 acres under cultivation, was totally fenced and the original grant of 120 acres was supplemented by a marsh of 25 acres. The original house was replaced by a 'capital two story brick dwelling house, lately finished in superior style, with cottage, out houses etc.'

Land in the area was selling at £30 per acre, and it was noted that vessels of 30 to 40 tons could berth within 100 yards of the house to load timber[3]. It was bought by a Mr. Robertson in March of that year at auction for £1100[4], an extremely high price reflecting its prestigious location and rich resources.

By 1837 the owner was John George Briggs, a wealthy retired Sea Captain owning several other properties in Hobart[5] and Launceston. He probably bought it from Mr. Robertson as they knew each other well[6]. Briggs lived on the estate with his wife and ten servants, but put it up for sale in May of 1838[7]. Elsewhere[8] he is credited with building the two story house, although it was apparently constructed at least 6 or 7 years earlier.

It's not clear who bought the farmland at this time and it is possible that parcels were sold off. Somewhere in the next few years the major part of the holding became known as "The Grove", the first public revelation of the name being in 1844 when another farmer used the land to auction off some of his farm assets[9]. A map of the area for 1840[10] shows the Montrose Farm estate being called "The Grove" and this may reflect Property and Valuation rolls for the period.

Captain John George Briggs died in 1844 elsewhere in the O'Brien's Bridge region[11]. His estate, apparently now smaller in size, was offered for sale in December 1847[12], being bought by John Providence Lester who was in residence by April 1849[13]. John's only daughter Mary Ann was married on the grounds[14] 14 Apr 1857 to John Hull, eighth son of another well-known family in the Tolosa region of what became Glenorchy. Lester subdivided the estate so that by the time of his death in 1867[15], The Grove was down to some 46 acres[16].

It is at this time that Stephen Peltro Henry Wright, recently from Glenelg, Adelaide, and already a resident of Glenorchy, stepped in and became the next owner of The Grove. One of his first acts was to pursue the suggestion of the Land agent and plant Hops. He advertised in the Mercury on Friday May 29 1868 and in September for appropriate resources.

Hops were grown up long poles, and whole families headed by the estate workmen's wives were involved at harvest time. Picking started at daylight, about half-past four, and continued all day. It was hard work, but the money was welcome, as there were few other ways for women to earn cash. At the end of harvest the pickers were paid off and the occasion was festive with parades in the streets.

By the end of 1868 Stephen had been elected as a Councillor of Glenorchy in recognition of his stature in the community[17].

Stephen was a determined man of industry. He now became a businessman farmer and invested not only in hops but also in apple trees. Hops required special drying kilns so he had some built, albeit with extra storage facilities that had unanticipated uses and benefits in later years. These became the largest kilns in Australia.

The Grove homestead had an enviable position in Glenorchy. The magnificent Georgian house had views from the rear of Mt. Wellington and views from the front of Mt. Direction across the Derwent river.

'Glenorchy Hills, Tasmania' by W.C. Piguenit. The Grove hop kilns appear to the left

By 1870 Stephen had enhanced the main house with formal gardens. This was a magnificent Georgian structure with adjoining buildings housing the kitchen, laundry and out-house facilities. Gardeners were employed to help maintain the residence and surrounds in beautiful condition. In 1874 his daughter Mona

The Grove
built circa. 1840
Artist: Mollie L. Tomlin

became the first to move away from home after marrying Henry Dunkin O'Halloran on 5th August[18].

Stephen became a member of Tasmania's Royal Society. Mrs. Wright ordered a number of plants in many lists from the Royal Society's Garden in Hobart. [The Royal Tasmanian Botanical Gardens.] Among her purchases in 1880 were 12 Giant Sequoia Redwoods (Wellingtonia) for 2 shillings each.

They appear in this 1940's aerial photo in which the house is circled.

On learning that Stephen had served as a member of the South Australian Board of Education the Tasmanian Government appointed him member of their Board of Education replacing Sir Robert Officer. Stephen's influence and importance grew.

The family now entered a highly volatile period. On 16 Jan 1882 Stephen's daughter Eva Dorinda married Winchester Munn Bisdee at St. Paul's Church of England in Glenorchy. Winchester's younger brother John was the first Tasmanian to be awarded the Victoria Cross for his services in the Boer War. He attained the rank of Colonel in World War I and received an O.B.E. in June 1919[19].

This was the first in a series of family marriages to take place over the coming years. Unfortunately before the next one could take place there was a sad event when Stephen's wife Elizabeth Jane died at home on 13 April 1884[20] aged 64 years old. Elizabeth had raised eight children born in two different countries and had been a wonderful mother and cheerful supporter of her husband and his business interests. Her role as instigator of local social events and leader of many charitable causes had helped establish the high regard with which the family was held in the community. Her passing was felt by family and local citizens alike.

Another death occurred four months later when Elizabeth's brother-in-law Edmund also aged 64 passed away on 5th August back in North Adelaide. Later in the year some rejuvenation occurred when Harold married Katherine Maria Chapman, daughter of the Premier, Thomas Daniel Chapman, in Hobart on 1st October[21]. And in 1885 Athol Howard was born to Winchester and Eva Bisdee 4 Feb, and Esmond Stephen Kennard was born to Harold and Katharine Wright 20 Sep. Despite these joyful events for the family, great sadness was to arrive the following year when the patriarch of The Grove, Stephen Peltro Henry Wright died on 15 Sep aged 67.

St. Pauls Anglican Church Montrose-Glenorchy

Here was the last of the original English Wrights to come to Australia. He followed his parents and brothers and sisters, rose to be Mayor of Glenelg, then moved his large family south to Glenorchy where he resurrected the social and business roles of a magnificent estate, developed major Hops and Apple plantations and gave his support to the growing community through council duties. Through 18 years in the district Stephen Wright was a leader in civic, business, and personal endeavours. He instilled pride and love in his family and his charitable acts endeared him to the community. His burial on 17th September was attended by farmers from towns up and down the Derwent, and by dignitaries from Hobart. He was buried alongside his wife in plot #67 at St. Paul's Anglican church Glenorchy[22].

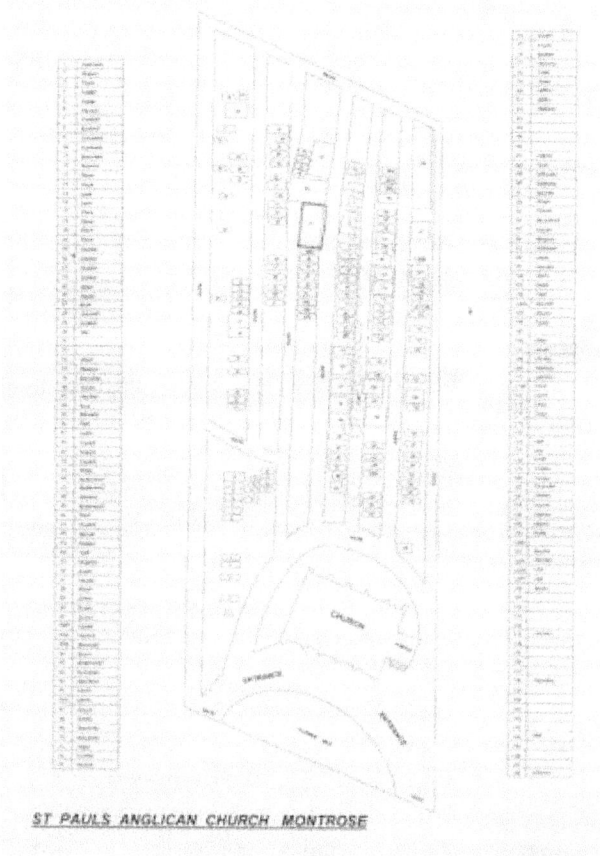

ST PAULS ANGLICAN CHURCH MONTROSE

XXX IN MEMORY

XX X XX

STEPHEN PELTRO HENRY WRIGHT

DIED 15TH SEPT^R. 1886.

AND ALSO OF

ELIZABETH JANE WRIGHT

WIFE OF ABOVE

DIED 16TH APRIL 1884

Less than a month after Stphen's death daughter Eva delivered her second child - Bernard Hutton Bisdee - on 10th October. About this time as the fortunes of The Grove grew, the remaining sons established The Wright Brothers Company, for the agricultural products they were now farming successfully. Their hops plantation was the largest in Tasmania. Harold became spokesman and leader of the estate initiatives. He followed in his father's footsteps in many ways – as an astute businessman, community supporter, and charitable social host of The Grove.

One of his first new efforts was to create a beautiful welcoming avenue of poplars along one of the entrances to the estate. And to invest further in the apple business with packing and storage sheds. Blessed with instinct Harold was the first grower to export apples to England. In the first batch the apples in all but one barrel arrived ruined, so Harold worked with shipping experts to successfully develop better packing and preservative methods and was eventually able to even 'brand' his apples by wrapping, which increased their value in London.

On 29 Jan 1888 sister Eva delivered her third child – Stephen John Bisdee - at Hutton Park, and later in the year on 24 Oct 1888 Harold's elder brother Howard married Maude Florence Rogers from Sydney at the Church of St. David in Hobart[23], where he lived in the house on Davey St. that his father had bought on arrival in Tasmania. In later years Maude and Howard became pillars of High Society in Hobart as Maude became chairperson of several charitable organizations. Their friends included the governor, a variety of successful business people, and other respected wealthy land owners.

Now it was Ernest's turn. On 8th June 1889 he married Kate Amelia Butler, daughter of the Honourable Henry Butler, at All Saint's Church, Glenorchy[24]. And in September Eva brought Dorothy Eva Bisdee into the world.

1890 was Harold's year. Early in the year he took up duties as the Warden of Glenorchy[25] and on June 14 his wife Katherine delivered a daughter – Kate Ione Howard. The Grove household was full of children's laughter and the fields were full of local citizens planting, managing and picking output from the biggest Apple and Hops farms in the country. Harold's uncle Edward Amand's death on 13 June the following year was a low point.

The late 1880s and the 1890+ decade were prosperous times for the Wright farming entity. Over 100 workers were engaged in the hop and apple business. Harold built eight 4-room cabins[26] on the estate for families who wanted to work for the Wright Bros. but had nowhere to live - an example of the type of action that endeared him to his workers. At the same time he built a sportsground and an 18 hole golf course "GroveLinks" for use by local citizens (including those in Hobart). He also helped form local Glenorchy cricket and football teams.

In late 1894, and early 1895, the Tasmanian Exhibition took place in Hobart. As members of the socially privileged upper class Howard and Harold and their wives were among those granted special season ticket passes. This international exhibition helped put Hobart 'on the map' so to speak. Its aim was 'to promote and foster industry, science, and art, by inciting the inventive genius of the people to a further improvement in arts and manufactures, as well as to simulate commercial enterprise by inviting all nations to exhibit their products both in the raw and finished state'[27].

The passes provided a mini photo album of family members:

Mr. Harold Stephen Robert Wright

Mrs. Katherine Maria (Chapman) Wright

Mr. Howard Edward Wright

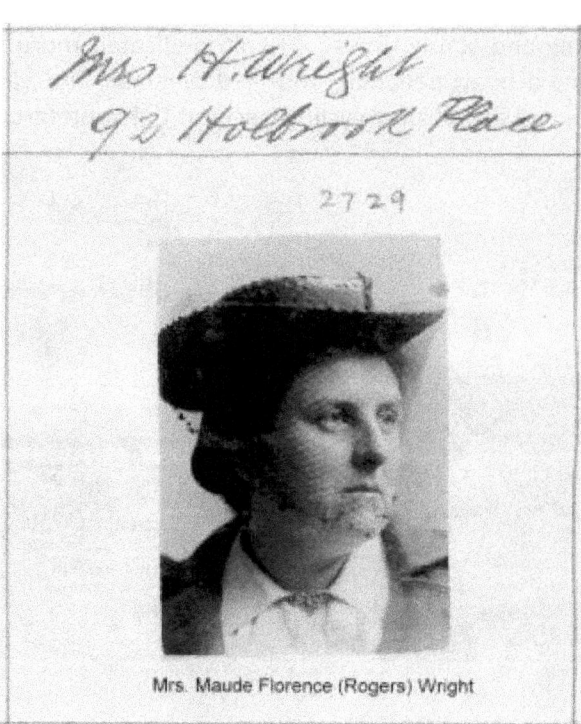

Mrs. Maude Florence (Rogers) Wright

The Grove by now was becoming the social centre of Glenorchy – and for that matter most of the surrounding area. Not only did workers benefit from wages, but their families were treated well. The Wrights were often asked to choose the name for a newborn. They contributed to the building and support of local churches[28], gave generously to local charities and created a community of like-minded farmers who made the region one of the most prosperous fruit-growing areas in the State.

Sadly, in Dec 1895, Harold's wife Katherine became ill and subsequently died, leaving a major hole in Harold's and the children's lives, especially having been married only 11 years[29] and young at only 45 years old. Harold carried on alone, and 27 months later his younger sister Nora Elizabeth married Arthur Edward Throne on 23 Mar 1898 at St. Paul's in Glenorchy. Young brother Bernard had moved into the banking world and was shortly to be appointed as a bank manager 150 miles NE of Glenorchy in St. Helen's. And Ernest, who had introduced apiaries[30] to generate honey for sale and to help the orchards back in 1886, had moved away as soon as he and Kate were married. Thus, Harold clearly became most strongly identified as the owner of the Grove, although the Wright Bros. was the trading entity, growing ever more successful as the company entered the twentieth century. One year the Wright Bros. sold 5,000 cases of apples, picked from 4.5 acres.

Federation in Australia, proclaimed January 1, 1901, instituted a Federal government and changed relationships between states so that in effect more completion ensued, especially in agriculture with the elimination of tariffs. The 'white Australia' policy effectively stopped the import of islanders for labour – especially in Queensland cane fields, and in part emboldened labour groups to push for greater consideration and recognition of value.

Despite the love and respect with which The Grove and the Wright family were held, the hop pickers called a strike in 1901, led by a Mrs. Fulton, demanding higher wages. While the workers won this round, Harold decided against planting hops the next season[31], and concentrated on apples only going forward. In the end the hops workers hurt themselves.

In 1902 on 5th December Harold married Mary Louisa Wayn at St. John's church, Toorak, Victoria[32]. Mary was the daughter of the Reverend Arthur Wayn and sister to Amelia Lucy Wayn who became an eminent Tasmanian historian. Mary came back to The Grove and helped Harold manage it through one of its more exciting and stable times. Harold dedicated more land from the estate for public use. He built a dock and bought a boat, becoming a skilled oarsman and yachtsman. He also arranged hunting parties for quail and snipe, and established cycling tracks at the sportsground[33].

C Class locomotive   http://www.railtasmania.com/photogal/showimage.php?id=384   Copyright Tasmanian Transport Museum

Harold's generosity and altruism were no better evidenced than when magnificent balls were staged in the Hop kilns. These balls could be instigated by all sorts of groups for various reasons. For appropriate causes Harold would even pay for a special train to be available to take passengers back to Hobart city after the revelling was over. The railway had cut through the property in 1876. It helped immensely with the speedy transport of packaged fruit to Hobart and beyond, and now Harold used it for convenience purposes as well[34]. This magnanimous behaviour on Harold's part endeared him to the community at large.

In 1910 on Aug 20 a bizarre accident occurred when Bernard, who now managed a property in Jericho 40 miles north of Glenorchy, was out riding on his horse and a large branch fell off a tree and killed him instantly[35]. Perhaps it was an omen for the times ahead. In 1914 a dispute emerged over water rights from Humphrey's rivulet, with farmers up and down the stream, along with the now well established tannery, seeking increased water use for crop irrigation and business purposes. A neighbour farmer, Joseph Cook, claimed he was losing income due to inadequate water availability and took his case to court in 1911 but lost. Harold followed in 1914 and similarly lost. He was forced to pay costs and take out a second mortgage to cover his financial position[36].

1917 however saw Harold starting to sell off estate resources. Draught horses, machinery, every-day farming implements and sadly, his 36ft yacht, along with the moorings. By 1919 the price of apples was being challenged in the market place. A large meeting of growers was held at the Grove on Thursday May 8 in which a floor price was set below which bag apples would not be sold to dryers, cider and jam factories. The farmers sought assistance from the Premier and set up a plan to unite all growers and their representatives across the state in an Association[37].

The Mercury, Thursday 10 May 1917 page 8

By 1920 neither the mainland nor Britain would take Tasmanian apples at a profitable price for growers and intermediaries. Many farmers started to subdivide their land and sell off building blocks as workers moved in to take jobs in the ever growing number of factories coming to the area[38].

The following years were not all kind. On 6 Sep 1924 Harold's elder brother Howard died in Hobart aged 75. The two had been very close for years, helping to build the business at the Grove and contribute to the community in the altruistic spirit of their father. Howard's passing was a devastating blow both to his wife Maude and to Harold[39].

And then just a few months later in April 1925 Harold's younger brother Ernest passed away at age 71. Harold was feeling quite alone. Son Esmond was in the news in October 1926 when a wheel on the car he was driving broke as he was turning a corner and flipped the car over. Amazingly, no-one was hurt and the car was light enough that bystanders were able to lift it upright[40].

Life on the estate continued without major change, except that in 1927 and 1928 apple prices suddenly picked up making life a bit more comfortable. On 27 July 1929 however Harold's sister-in-law Maude died in Hobart[41], leaving a sizeable estate, to be shared with friends and relatives in Hobart, Sydney and South Australia, as well as portions for select charities[42].

By 1931 outlying areas of The Grove estate were sold off so that other growers now used "The Grove" address as well[43]. The family's wealth shown in Maude's will was also displayed when her husband's mammoth library of over 2,000 volumes was sold off that year[44]. Very sadly Harold's second wife Mary Louisa died in December the following year[45]. Clearly Harold himself had some excellent longevity genes as he had now outlived most of his siblings and two wives.

Many of the Wrights seemed to marry later in life and Harold's son Esmond was no exception. He married Ethel Longmore 4 Mar 1933[46] in Hobart at the age of 47, with the reward of a son Kennard Robert George arriving 25 January 1934[47]. Still active on the estate in 1935 Harold attended the opening of The Grove Esplanade, a 2.25 acre reserve from the estate subdivision on the banks of the Derwent especially set aside for the children of Glenorchy[48].

By 1940 at age 89 however Harold no longer had the energy to look after The Grove. Further subdivision of the land was imminent and so he started the process of closing things down with a sale of redundant farm equipment[49] and his own relocation to Sandy Bay at his son Esmond's home there. Daughter Kate, unmarried, stayed on.

In 1941 Harold's sister Eva died at the age of 82 and shortly after on 4th January 1842 Harold himself passed away in a private hospital in Hobart[50]. The Mercury on Jan 7 1942 p5 published an obituary describing the public tribute accorded Harold at his cremation.

Harold's death in some ways signalled the end of an era. He had lived at The Grove for 72 years. The Grove's role in hops and apple production was pivotal to the State's agricultural development. The magnanimity of the Wright family over the years had created a reverence and love in the wider Glenorchy community unmatched by any other local family. While many of the Wrights had married into High Society they never forgot the common folks who tilled their land, picked the crops, or birthed their children on the estate. Land was donated for sports and other recreational facilities and open to all. This pioneering family, while happily well-off, had also brought prosperity to many - not just the workers on the estate per se, but to the owners and employees of all the commercial facets of the emergent apple-related industry – from canneries to rail transportation to mercantile shipping. From landed gentry in South Australia a century earlier the sharp business acumen and creative innovation inherent in the Wright genes had made a remarkable impact in the fair state of Tasmania. From local politics to business dealings the Wrights had definitely served their fellow man well.

OBITUARY

MR. H. S. R. WRIGHT

Public Tribute At Cremation

Representatives of the Glenorchy municipality, in which much of his active life was spent, were present at the Cornelian Bay cemetery yesterday, at the service which preceded the cremation of Mr Harold S. R. Wright, formerly of The Grove, Glenorchy who died on Sunday at Hobart in his 91st year. The service was conducted by the Rev. L. F. Benjafield. The chief mourners were the deceased's son, Mr. Esmond R. Wright, his grandson, K. R. Wright, and his nephews, Mr. A. H. Bisdee, Mr. S. J. Bisdee, and Mr. B. H. Bisdee who was accompanied by Mrs Bisdee, and Mr G R Chapman. The Glenorchy Commission (the deceased was formerly Warden of the municipality) was represented by the chairman (Mr H L Batten), Mr J D Hickey (associate commissioner), Mr C Henry (secretary), and the municipal engineer (Mr J L Fowler). The Rev L A Burgess, rector of St Paul's Church, Glenorchy, and Mr L. R. Turner, a warden of the church, were present. Mr E. M. Johnson, K.C., represented the Tasmanian Club, of which the deceased was a member for 60 years. Others at the service were Messrs E H Webster, J Swan (Brighton), M. H. Swan, and E Jones. The cremation arrangements were conducted by Alex Clark and Son Ltd.

Life at the Estate moved slowly on as it downsized considerably, and after Harold's daughter Kate died in a private hospital in Hobart on Jan 4th 1949[51] it was put up for sale and bought by a local Glenorchy resident Mr. Bert Mollineaux.

Finally, after 80 years in the possession of the Wrights, The Grove was owned by outsiders. From initially being well over 100 acres in size with a commanding and highly desirable location on the banks of the Derwent and Humphreys Rivulet, on three sides it was now bordered by small farms and housing developments.

The original beauty was gone, only a remnant remaining to support the memory banks of older local residents and aging Wright family members living elsewhere.

When only 8 or so acres were left after further blocks were sold, the owner authorized A.G. Webster and sons to sell all that remained.   The property was advertised in the Mercury Saturday 17 Nov 1951 p22.

WEDNESDAY, DECEMBER 5
GLENORCHY PROPERTY

Are favoured with instructions from the owner, Mr. B. Mollineaux, to offer for sale by Public Auction, at their Mart, Liverpool St., Hobart, on the above date at noon:—

ALL THAT valuable property situate at Glenorchy, known as "The Grove," comprising a substantially built brick residence on stone foundations, with iron roof, containing 9 rooms and conveniences. Most of the fittings are of cedar, and main rooms have open fireplaces and power points. Numerous brick outbuildings, some of which are in need of repair Large workshop with electric light and power points on separate meters from house. Included in the sale is one glass house of approx. 45ft. x 15ft., fitted with electric hotbox.   There is a picturesque brick wall 170ft. long and 9ft. high extending into the garden.   One 4-roomed W.B. cottage with electric light and power points and conveniences is occupied by a tenant at £1 per week. The buildings and portion of the garden are supplied by water from the Glenorchy Council main.

The land comprises an area of 8 acres 1 rood 19 3/10 perches, and is bounded on the east or south-east by Humphreys Rivulet; together with a right-of-way 50ft. wide leading to the main road, and a right-of-way 50ft. wide at the rear leading to Grove Rd.   The land is first-class growing land, level and most suitable for horticultural work or poultry farming.   The property would be suitable for racing stables or a stud farm, being only half a mile from the Elwick Racecourse and Showground, and it would be equally suitable for industrial purposes or as a subdivision proposition.   Good transport facilities by rail, tram, or bus services.

At present there are many fruit and English ornamental trees on the property. This is an opportunity which rarely occurs for an investor or anyone requiring a comparatively large area close to the city.

TERMS: 10 p.c. deposit, balance on completion, and if required first mortgage can be arranged.
POSSESSION: Vacant Possession, 1st March, 1952.
TITLE: Correct.
REFERENCE: Messrs. Butler, McIntyre, and Butler, Solicitors, Hobart.
Arrangements to inspect made with Auctioneers or direct with owner.

3 months later in February 1952 a clearing sale of excess farm implements, furniture – even two boats – took place[52], and to all intents and purposes The Grove was gone, and its land was re-zoned for purely commercial purposes. Surrounding streets received memorable names – Peltro, Wrights, Grove etc but they hardly reflected the splendour once present.

All in all, an ignominious ending to a once magnificent estate.

Author's note: Here ends the story of The Grove per se. No other single entity played such a prominent and important role in the development of Glenorchy. The name Glenorchy is believed to have originated with governor Lachlan Macquarie. His wife came from Glen Orchy – a glen containing the river Orchy in Scotland.

One wonders why no Wright relatives wanted to own and manage The Grove after Kate's death in 1949. Perhaps its urbanization was too difficult to accept given the loss of the natural habitat with which most would have grown up.

Today (early 2011) the original residence stands in ruins inside a timber yard. What little is known about its history over the past 50 years or so, plus some incidental learnings about the family, are described in the following chapter.

Chapter 3: Miscellany

The Mansion at The Grove

It's difficult to determine the history of the house at The Grove once the Wright family departed. It's possible that for a while it was rented out by the new owners, who continued to keep it somewhat intact. Clearly however as modern conveniences became more available there was a need to update the dwelling and no-one took on that obligation. Its historic value was clearly recognized and so it was left alone but not cared for. At some point in the 1960s Chinese gardeners planted vegetables and supplied local markets with produce. But the house started to disintegrate and became unsuitable for living.

The outbuildings were torn down and the roof was exposed in rusty state. Broken window panes were not replaced and the front door was boarded up. The flower gardens went to seed. A large lone tree grew up providing early morning shade, but the grandeur was sadly gone and what ended up remaining was just a relic of a glorious past.

And somewhere in the 1980s vandals broke in and created a fire, burning all the timber framework inside and causing the roof to cave in, so that all remained were the original brick walls and chimneys.

By this time this part of the original estate was owned by the McKay family – well-known timber merchants.

Lacking attention and open to the elements, invasive plant varieties seeded inside and before long extensive shrubbery became established, with roots creating pressure on interior walls and arches so that cracks occurred, window ledges collapsed, and in some cases whole walls caved in.

With less woodwork support the chimneys collapsed next, in some cases taking part of the walls with them. Concrete window ledges fell and split, electrical wires and plumbing pipes were exposed.

Yet, even in its saddened state today some of the craftsmanship and quality of the building is evident.

Front facing Mt. Direction

and rear facing Mt. Wellington

These poplar trees stand on the eastern side of Humphrey's Rivulet, off the estate, and are a reminder of the avenue of poplars that helped serve as a windbreak for the hop fields 100 years or so earlier

Thick plastering and solid door frames were standard

The brick work is in a style called 'Flemish bond'[1] in which every second brick is placed end on so that the wall is double the usual thickness and provides added strength. This is probably the reason the house survived the fire so well and has stood for so long – now close to 180 years.

The location of the house in Glenorchy today is depicted in the following map by the letter H.

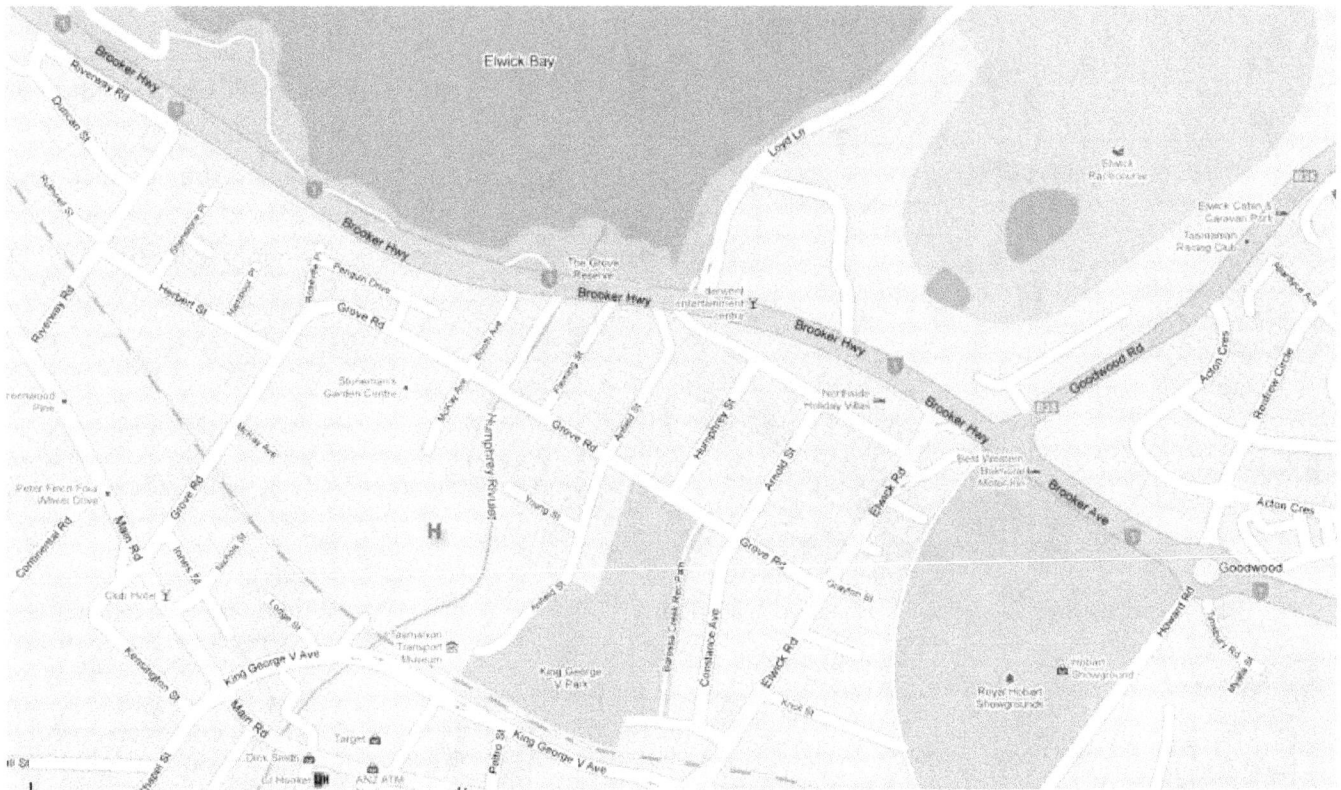

The only entrance is through McKay's timber yard to the South at the end of Wrights avenue, off King George V Ave.

The Grove plantings

From the earliest of times there was note of plantings at The Grove. In 1821 there was "a Garden well stocked with choice Fruit Trees" (see Footnote 2 of Chapter 2). By 1870 there were well established formal flower gardens in front of the dwelling. Poplar trees had been planted along an entrance avenue and were also used as a windbreak for the hops fields. Starting in 1875, Mrs. Stephen Wright bought shrubs from the Royal Society's Garden. Her husband Stephen was a member of the Royal Society, hence the ability to be able to purchase plants from the Royal Society's Garden, (now the Royal Tasmanian Botanical Gardens). Early lists in

Abbott's Account Sales book (private communication from Mrs. Gwenda Sheridan) show a large number of Box plants seen in the small box hedges in the photograph of the house above.

On 17th June 1879 Mrs. Wright bought a Wellingtonia sequoia, and followed this order on 16th February 1880 with an order for 11 more at a cost of 2 shillings (2/-) each. At this date this was a very substantial order and shows the commitment that Elizabeth Jane had for beautifying The Grove. The Grove was so prominent that this sort of action established standards for other estates.

The railway line that bifurcated the estate, but which became so valuable for efficient freight and people transportation, no doubt also received some plantings to help shield its presence. In the 1940s photo at left shielding by *Cupressus macrocarpa* is seen to the north of the line in neighbouring properties. The foliage along the rivulet is probably *Pittosporum undulatum* as Mrs. Wright had ordered 12 of these trees at one stage and the 1940s photo trees are likely descendants.

The large tree immediately to the northwest of the house is also seen in both the photo above as well as in the first image shown in this chapter. And of course originally much of the grounds were taken up with the apple orchard. Trees, gardens, flowers were a way of life at The Grove. The choice of trees bought by Mrs. Wright shows a discerning knowledge of plants in general – no doubt influencing other well-to-do estate owners.

Wright family friends

The Wrights clearly ran in High Society circles. Stephen and son Harold were both Mayor of Glenorchy at different times. Stephen had connections in Sydney from his time as Mayor of Glenelg. He sat on Educational Advisory Committees, was a member of Tasmania's Royal Society, and became a leader in the emergent Apple industry. Harold married the Tasmanian premier's daughter Katherine Chapman and later Maria Wayn, sister of noted historian Amelia. One of the sisters is depicted here in 1894.

Harold's brother Ernest Wright married Kate Butler, from an historically prominent Tasmanian family, daughter of the respected parliamentarian the Honorable Henry Butler. Sister Eva Dorinda Wright married Winchester Bisdee. His mother was Ellen Jane Butler, sister of Henry, so Ernest and Eva actually married spouses who were cousins.

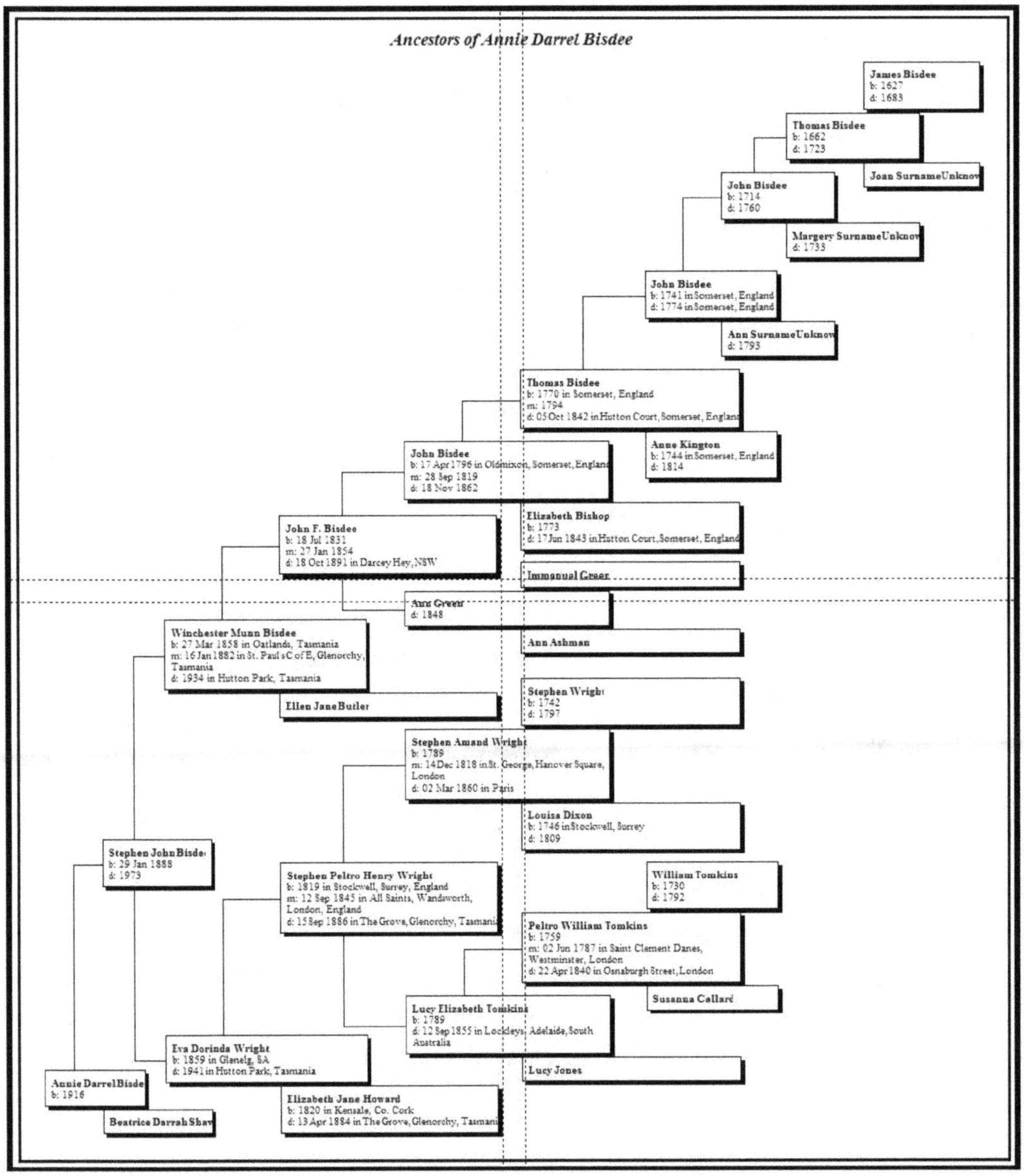

In the Bisdee family, Winchester's younger brother by 11 years, John, became quite famous as a soldier. On 26 April 1900 at the age of 30 he sailed from Tasmania and served in operations in Cape Colony, the Transvaal and the Orange River Colony. On 1 September, near Warmbad, Transvaal, he was with a scouting party ambushed by Boers in a rocky defile; six of the eight men in the party were wounded, including an officer whose horse broke away and bolted. Bisdee dismounted, put the wounded man on his own horse and ran alongside, then mounted behind him and withdrew under heavy fire. For this action he received the Victoria Cross—the first

Governor of Tasmania awarding VC to John Bisdee

awarded to a Tasmanian. Wounded during the ambush, he was invalided home but, on recovering, went back to South Africa as a lieutenant in No.1 Company, 2nd Tasmanian Imperial Bushmens' Contingent, and served from March 1901 until the end of the war. After serving in many other theatres he was appointed a major in the Australian Military Forces in 1915, was placed on reserve in 1921 and on the retired list, with the honorary rank of lieutenant-colonel, in 1929.

John Bisdee with family in front of house

John Bisdee welcome home train

Bisdees, Butlers and Wrights became intertwined families. Lots of other relationships emerged over the years.

North and west of The Grove the Lowes family had established a farm and residence called Lowestoff in Berriedale. By the time the Wrights were in place this beautiful estate was owned by the Cameron family. See Footnote 28 in Chapter 2. The Camerons were Glenorchy community supporters like the Wrights.

Other neighbour friends included the Shoobridges.

Lowestoff, Berriedale, Tasmania

They also were apple growers – essentially in competition with the Wright Brothers. Harold in his 1940 recollections indicated the friendly rivalry in claims over which family first exported apples to England. See Footnote 27, Chapter 1.

Ebenezer Shoobridge (1820-1901), was a pioneer agriculturalist of Glenora and later member of the Tasmanian Legislative Council. He and his wife Charlotte, née Giblin, had 3 sons – William Ebenezer (1846-1940), politician, agriculturalist and industrial innovator, Robert Wilkins Giblin (1847-1936), agriculturalist and innovator, and Louis Manton (1852-1939), agriculturalist, politician and Nature lover. William developed an irrigation system for hops and apples which overcame the dryness of the deep porous soil and allowed extensive cultivation of such hop varieties as Early White Grape, Goldings, Green Grape and Red Golding. Over the period 1866-79 the acreage trebled and the crop increased sevenfold, becoming the basis of an important export industry. Within the apple industry William encouraged production of Sturmers, Pippins and Nonpareils for the London market, developing the 'cup' pattern technique of pruning the vigorous, irrigated crop.

Robert and Louis were also prominent inventors in agriculture. Robert took over Valleyfield estate near New Norfolk, producing an annual apple crop of 40,000 bushels. He had a particular interest in cool storage: as president of the Fruitgrowers' Association he travelled to London with a cargo of apples, advising on storage and critical temperatures, to establish standard shipboard conditions. Louis was president of the Agricultural Council, Royal Agricultural Society, Tasmanian Farmers' and Stock Owners' Association and the Australian Pomological Committee, as well as chairman of the National Park Board and member of many other societies. His most enduring achievement however stemmed from his selection and preservation of fifty acres near the beautiful Russell Falls. The site was proclaimed part of an enlarged 300-acre reserve in 1885 and in 1917 was incorporated into the 27,000 acre Mt Field National Park.

Some flavour of the Shoobridge milieu is conveyed by the annual strawberry feast the Shoobridges held for their workers at the famous Bushy Park hop-barn which 'had Biblical texts on its outer walls and was frequently used as a church on Sundays. The hop-picking was always closed with a festival in true Kentish style. Poles garlanded with hops and bedecked with coloured ribbons, were carried around in procession amid wild cheering. A dinner, with music and song brought the day to its close'. The strength of the family tradition is also preserved in the inscription of the original hop kiln built by Ebenezer Shoobridge and known as the 'Text Kiln' from the Biblical texts also engraved on it, which reads 'Erected by Ebenezer Shoobridge, 1867, assisted by his wife and three sons and five daughters. Union is Strength'.

Howard and his brothers Ernest and Harold played football for the local New Town team in the early 1880s but once he moved south of Glenorchy to Hobart and married Maude Rogers, Howard and his wife cultivated friends in high places. They were a strongly religious couple, contributing much to charities and worthwhile causes – both financially, in goods, and in personal effort. Families like the Braddons, Patersons, Butlers, Adams, Overells, Howards, Evans, and Whitingtons became good friends, with many of the women joining Maude in officer positions in various societies such as the Red Cross Society, Union Jack Society caring for wounded soldiers, and the Anchor Club looking out for less privileged families[2].

Public activities were frequently described in the Mercury, showing their wide associations and participation in worthy causes. In some cases their presence at a Government levee – such as that arranged for the visit of the Duke and Duchess of Cornwall's visit in July 1901 (See p3 of The Mercury Friday 5 July 1901) – would be noted. They sometimes travelled to Sydney and attended similar events there, Howard having business associates there and of course Maude having family.

Mrs. V. Butler lived nearby at 8 Elboden St. on the corner of Holebrook Place. She and the Overell sisters, neighbours on Holebrook Place, were close friends. Lilian as a spokesperson for women's rights and worthwhile local civic causes clearly had a strong admirer in Maude[3]. While obviously a well-regarded and intelligent couple, perhaps Howard and Maude were not always as practical as others. Both at different times lost their pet dogs and advertised rewards for finders in the local papers.

One can only surmise that the rewards were very worthwhile.

One of the dogs appears in the photo of the steps in the next section.

Holebrook Place and Davey St. – Location of Howard and Maude Wright's home

In 1894 Maude and Howard lived at 92 Holebrook Place, which is where Howard's father first lived on arrival in Hobart from South Australia. Howard actually owned several other residences in Holebrook place and Davey St. and was a shrewd real-estate investor. Davey St. and Holebrook Place were where the cream of Hobart society lived at the end of the 19th and start of the 20th century. In 1912 when the Rosny development was instigated, plans included a road to match the style and legend of Davey St and Holebrook Place[4]. Holebrook Place was essentially the upper end of Davey St. running from Elboden Place/St. to Lynton Ave (at one time called Reform St.) intersecting Holebrook opposite Darcy St.

By the 1920s homes in Holebrook Place had been given numbers that extended those of Davey St and gradually Holebrook Place per se faded out of common usage[5]. 92 Holebrook Place became 244 Davey St.[6]

The following maps of 1890s vintage from the Tasmanian State Library show original plans and naming.
http://catalogue.statelibrary.tas.gov.au/item/?q=NOT+series%3aSTORS&format=Images+%5c+Map&avail=Online&tas=Tasmanian&i=3&id=868675

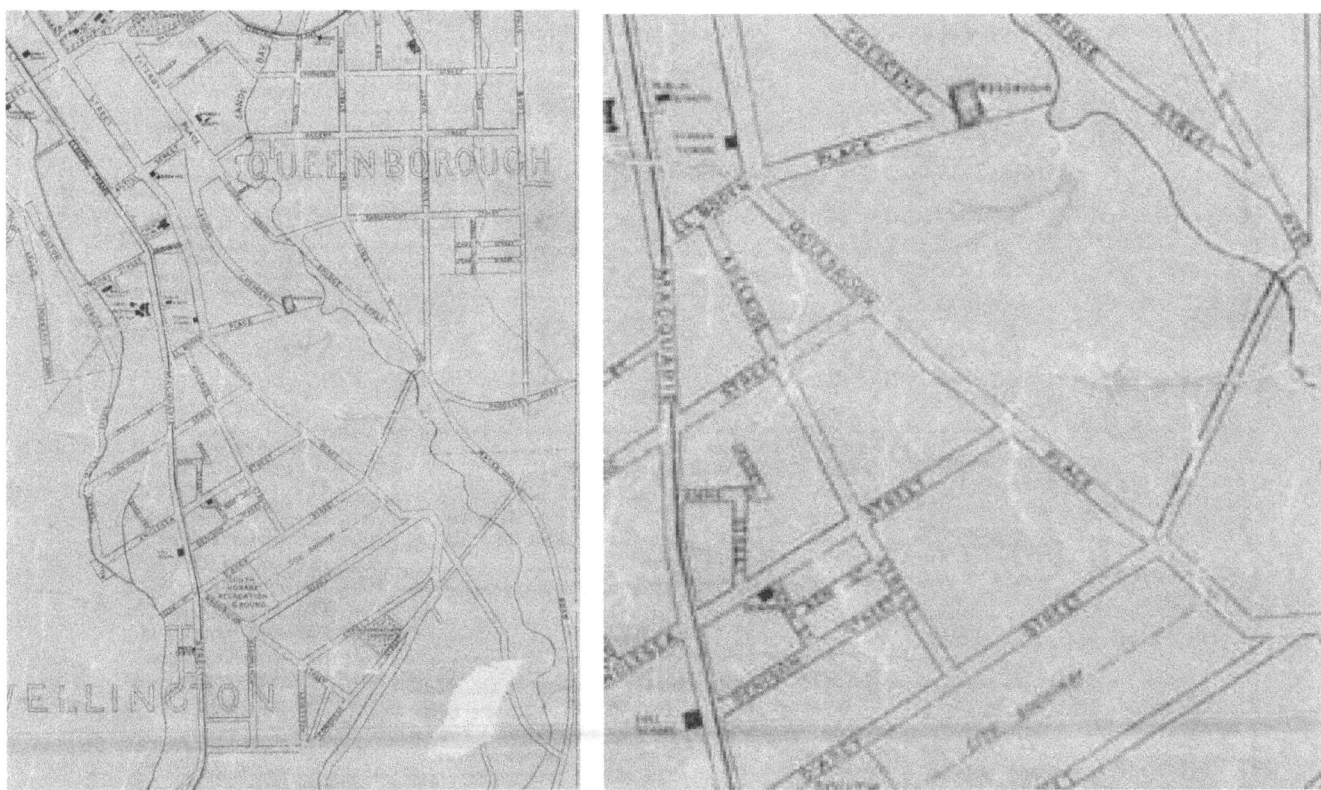

Somewhere during the second world war as the beautiful properties along Davey St., became subdivided and innumerable new houses were added, the numbering changed yet again and by 1945 # 244 Davey St. was # 328 Davey St., as it is today[7].

Back in 1894/5 seven large estates took up the 1700 feet of frontage along Holebrook Place. At the top of the hill on the Derwent side was the house of Sir William Lambert, the Chief Justice[8]. Next to it on substantial acreage was "The Priory" in which Maude and Howard Wright lived. They never used the house name per se but always referred to their home as 92 Holebrook Place, even after the first renumbering took effect.

```
Postal Directory 1894-5 Page_76 Holebrook place Wright Howard.jpg

         142 Atkins Mrs. Emma
         144 Pearce Mrs. John
         ........ here is Arthur st ........

            Hobart Rivulet, Cascades.
         Dodge William T
         Proctor Thomas
         Hursey James

              Holebrook place.
         Right hand side from Davey st.
         Riordan Mrs. E. T
         Browne Thomas A
         Ritchie A. McDonald
         Walch James H. B. (Walch &
            Sons) (Hillcrest)
         Giblin Mrs. Thomas
         ...... here is city boundary ......
         Left hand side from City boundary.
            WebsterAlfd.G (Webster&Son)
            Maxwell Crawford J.(Leswalt)
            Chapman George S. (Waruna)
            Walker Cecil (Lindfield)
         84 WebsterMrs.G.A.(Beauregard)
            Wright Howard
            Dobson Hon. Sir Wm.Lambert
            M.E.C. (Chief Justice)
         ...... here is city boundary ......

            Hope street.
```

In *Mansions, Cottages and All Saints*. Drawings by Audrey Holiday and Text by Walter Eastman. Printing Authority of Tas. Hobart 1994 on page 8 we learn of some unusual history of The Priory.

> "The man who built this tall three-storey house of red colonial brick was no stranger to sadness, adventure and perhaps more than a little villainy.
>
> Hugh Cokeley Ross, barrister, solicitor and conveyancer arrived in the Colony of Van Diemens Land in December, 1822, on board the Regalta, and was admitted to the Lieut-Governor's Court on April lst, the following year. He was admitted to the Supreme Court the very next day. His ownership of the land on which The Priory now stands was twelve years into the future.
>
> He and a legal partner were solicitors to the Bank of Van Diemens Land when it was formed in August, 1823.
>
> He suffered a bitter blow in 1825 when his 26-year-old wife, Sarah, mother of their four small children, died and was buried in what is now St. David's Park.
>
> By 1835, when he had purchased what was then a very large block of land where The Priory stands today, he was acting as Crown Solicitor for the Colony, and had married again. His second wife of six years standing was Anna Maria, and she would eventually bear him four sons.
>
> His newly acquired land had a frontage on Davey Street and extended down to the Sandy Bay Rivulet near to what is now King Street. The area was "3 acres, 2 roods and 25 perches"-about 1 ½ hectares. The man from whom be bought it- a Commander in the Royal Navy, one Charles Colville Frankland Esq. -had built a cottage on it. Ross then set about changing it to "an elegant and spacious residence" of one storey and consisting of at least six rooms. There is evidence in the present structure that the servants lived in the roof.

In February, the year after Ross took possession, HMS Beagle arrived in Hobart Town with a young naturalist on board by the name of Charles Darwin. Darwin spent much time with another Frankland, the better known George, the surveyor with whom Governor Arthur had a long standing disagreement. George Frankland owned the block next door to Ross's developing mansion, and from Darwin's diary it appeared he walked past the Ross house on his way to Mt. Wellington.

Sadly, by 1840, Ross was in Financial difficulties and the following notice appeared in the Hobart Town Gazette of 11th December that year; about an "Elegant and Spacious Family Residence":

to be sold without the least reserve...the very convenient, substantial and elegantly furnished FAMILY RESIDENCE. together with the Garden ...stocked with every variety of the choicest and most valuable shrubs, fruit and forest trees, flowers, bulbs etc., in the collection of which no expense has been spared.

The reason given for the sale, without reserve, was Ross's "professional engagements requiring his constant residence in Town." (!) Worse was to come. Because of the current financial climate in the Colony the fine house brought £1,000 less than expected and, a month later, the Hobart Town Courier carried this story:

A great sensation has been occasioned by the absconding of Mr. Hugh Ross, the Crown Solicitor, with, it is said, a considerable sum of the public money and various have been the rumours and conjectures afloat respecting the mode in which be affected his escape...

He was eventually caught, returned to the Colony and acquitted on a technicality. In the late l8S0's, The Priory was bought by a city chemist, Henry Hinsby, who added the second floor. In 1864, he completed its construction by adding the attic bedrooms. Present owners [1994], Clive and Linda Newton, confirm that the first floor verandah on the southern side is still -in the words of the press advertisement of more than a century and a half ago -"commanding a most delightful view of the harbour and Sandy Bay." [End of copy]

Like all the houses on Holebrook Place The Priory (at top left centre in this photo) was a magnificent dwelling. The gardens were extensive and the front faced the Derwent River with panoramic views to the north, east and south. A small orchard grew on the slope down to Sandy Bay.

The house was built with orange bricks, just like The Grove in Glenorchy, probably adding to the comfort for the Wrights with both. A fountain played in front and sandstone steps led to entrances. The beauty of the house is still evident today as shown by this side and partial front photo

The current location of the house was determined by comparing 1947 Hobart Drainage maps with present day Google and Bing aerial photos[9]. The left photo below shows the unusual roof style and the location of the original fountain to the front right of the main entrance. The right photo shows the privacy hedge of *C. torulosa* cypresses in front of the house and the old stables, now a residence, behind.

Maude and Howard were known for their generosity. 92 Holebrook Place was a house of substantial proportions, for international and interstate visitors were often accommodated there. Maude especially had a kind heart and a sincere penchant for helping others. During the 1914-1919 war years she and Howard opened up their house to recuperating soldiers who had been discharged from hospital but still needed recovery therapy. One can only imagine how the amazing views, the beautiful gardens, and the peaceful surroundings must have aided the process of regaining health.

Beyond Lynton Ave further uphill on Davey St., Howard's brother Ernest built his residence just a few doors away as seen in the 1919 and later directory listings. And brother Harold's son Esmond, who married Ethel Longmore in 1933, established a residence nearby in Sandy Bay.

Clearly the Wright family was closely knit and enjoyed both the Glenorchy area and the south of Hobart in the upper Davey St/Sandy Bay area.

Quamby – an Aboriginal name for 'place of rest'

A little northeast of Hagley on the Meander River is the estate known as Quamby. From 500 acres originally granted to Richard Dry in 1819 the estate grew to 30,000 acres (extending as far northwest as Quamby Bend) and after subdivision still today commands a gorgeous presence due to over 12 acres of beautiful gardens, hothouses and parklands.

A son, Sir Richard Dry, was a member of the Royal Society and in 1860 obtained an extensive list of plants from what is now the Royal Tasmanian Gardens. While primarily a list of shrubs, herbs, roses, flowering perennials and annuals, the list also contained an elm, maples, ailanthus, Huon pine, the false myrtle-beech (*Nothofagus cunninghamii*), a Silky Oak, a Japanese cedar and willows. The list gives an excellent insight into what plants were then available at this time from the Royal Society for distribution; plants which were fashionable (e.g. fuchsia, verbena), or for medicinal or household use (e.g. tansy, golden rod, tobacco), or had pretty showy flowers (e.g. aster, delphinium, gazania, phlox, salvia). Twelve gardeners are reputed to have managed the gardens and Sir Richard Dry won (or his gardeners did) a number of prizes at the Launceston Horticultural Show over the years including prizes for geraniums, fuchsias, pelargoniums, calceolarias, roses, green house plants. The Gardener's Cottage was located just south of the two large *C. deodar* trees on the golf course, and the orchard was directly behind that.

As late as 1860 some 800 people still lived on the estate. Among the employees was the Dent family – they were the coachmen for Sir Richard Dry[10]. By 1887 nearly 18,000 acres of the original property had been sold off, yet the magnificence remained. That gradually deteriorated over time until the Barnett family bought the property in 1955 and held it for 35 years. They restored the house and grounds which had fallen into considerable disrepair, re-invigorating gardens and planting new trees. The present golf course was developed by owners who followed the Barnett family so is of relatively recent origin. The old trees (oaks, elms, redwoods, some remaining conifers along the drive, remnant conifers on the golf course) are a reminder of, and a significant contribution to, the micro landscape which is Quamby in 2010.

An earlier owner just prior to the Barnetts was Lady Sallie Ferrall. Before the Southern Outlet was built in Hobart a lot of subdivision and demolishing took place along the upper end of the prestigious Davey St. Lady

Ferrall remembers that the original fountain at Quamby was broken and that she and her husband bought a close replica from a house in Holebrook Place. The huge house downhill next to The Priory and its associated land was one of the victimized properties and while The Priory remained intact, the fountain there disappeared, its old position still evident in photos today. While no specific proof is available it is conjectured that the original fountain at the Priory now resides at Quamby[11].

The old and new fountains, while similar, were quite distinct.

Old Quamby fountain

New Quamby fountain ex Holebrook Place, Hobart

Maude (Rogers) Wright's Will

Howard Wright married Maude Rogers in Hobart on 24 Oct 1888. Howard was senior to Maude by 11 years. They had no children.

The couple lived at 92 Holebrook Place, Hobart. Howard died from a serious illness on 6 Sep 1924, a month short of his 75th birthday. His obituary is taken from the Mercury Monday 8 Sep 1924, p6.

Five years later Maude was also an invalid requiring attention at home. From the Mercury Tuesday 25 June 1929 p1

> WANTED, middle-aged person, to look after invalid at night. Apply, with references, to 92 Holebrook Place.

Roughly a month later Maude died of a heart attack at her home. (244 Davey St. = 92 Holebrook Place)

TASMANIA
The Births, Deaths and Marriages Registration Act 1909

RECORD OF DEATH — Registration No. 1690/1929

1. Surname of deceased: WRIGHT
2. Christian or other names: Maude Florence
3. Date of death: 27 JULY 1929
4. Place of death: 244 Davey St, HOBART
5. Occupation: Not Stated
6. Stated year of birth/age at death: 68 years
7. Sex: FEMALE
8. Usual place of residence: Not Stated
9. Reputed birthplace: SYDNEY
10. Conjugal condition at death: WIDOWED
11. If ever married - Name and surname of last spouse: Howard WRIGHT
12. Issue - of all marriages: Living males / Living females / Deceased males / Deceased females
13. Age at each marriage: 26 years (first) / (second) / (third) / (etc)
14. If never married - names of parents:
15. If born overseas - Period of residency in Australia:
16. Date registered: 29 JULY 1929
17. Registration officer/district: J.P. LAUGHTON

ENDORSEMENT(S)
Formerly recorded as: D H 1874 1929 F in District HOBART

Cause of Death: PHTHISIS / CARDIAC FAILURE
Medical Attendant: DR. R. WHISHAW
Informant: A J CLARK, UNDERTAKER, COLLINS ST

Mr. Howard Edward Wright, of Holebrook Place, a well-known Hobart citizen, died at his residence on Saturday, after a severe illness. Mr. Wright had taken a prominent part in the prospecting and exploration of the West Coast in his younger days, and he was also well known as an orchardist. He was the eldest son of the late Mr. Stephen Wright, of Adelaide, and coming to Hobart with his parents at an early age, was for some time resident at "The Grove," Glenorchy. He was at one time a member of the Fisheries Board, and also took a keen interest in sport, and was connected in his youth with the New Town Football Club, while his name was not unknown in rowing circles. Of late years he had made a hobby of raising pedigree poultry. Mr. Wright married Miss Maud Rogers, a daughter of the late Judge Rogers of New South Wales, who survives him, but had no children. He was a brother of Mr. Harold Wright, of "The Grove," Glenorchy, and of Mr. Ernest Wright, while his sisters, Mrs. Winchester Bisdee and Miss Wright, also survive him. The funeral service will be held at All Saints Church to-morrow morning, commencing at 10.30 o'clock, and immediately afterwards the funeral will move to St. John's churchyard, New Town, arriving at 11.30.

By all measures of the period Maude was very well off at the time of her death leaving behind a sizeable estate, much of which was in real estate holdings. Unfortunately the national depression was not far behind making it hard to dispose of land and houses and it took over 9 years to finally conclude estate matters.

One of these holdings was the property named "Ellington" in Sandy Bay. At some point the Lipscombe family, of Nursery fame, lived there.

Maude's will is reproduced in the Footnotes[12] and salient points are listed below. The only mention of her husband Howard is in a request that all the Silver in the home be given to a Rev. Henry Howard, resident in Blenheim, NZ. No further information on Rev Howard is available.

In terms of goods and chattels the teapot went to Alice Bowring (possibly a maid), 3 boxes and a camphor trunk in the attic to Madge Overell, a paisley shawl to her niece Alice Rogers, her lace to be split evenly between Alice and Lilian Overell, her diamond ring, 3 little tables and 3 lacquer tables to go to Lilian, curios and pictures to Louisa Overell, while the hall dresser was for Florie Owens in Victoria, and 3 pieces of china to Rosalie Shaw. These gifts show what was important and valuable in Society at the time. The books were to go to the Ladies College in Sydney – a forerunner of the Presbyterian Ladies College there.

Maude's instructions were to sell her real estate holdings including frontage on her street with special recognition for access to one gentleman's property behind one of the lots. Funds realized were then to be divided up and given to a number of friends as follows:

Mary Whitington £1000, £500 to each of brother in law Ernest, niece Alice, Alice Maude Turner, Rev. T. K. Pitt, Isabel Corlette, Hugh Williams, and Arthur Daintry. £250 to each of Clara Camilla Ogilvy and Kenneth Arthur Ogilvy, £300 to Amy Shaw and Kitty Hudspeth, £125 each to the 4 misses Adams, with £100 going to each of 9 others. A total of £7,000. The Reserve Bank of Australia[13] suggests this would be the equivalent of about $460,000 in 2009 currency, although the author considers this to be probably less than half the actual effective value.

Anything left over was to be divided as follows: a quarter to the Australian Board of Missions in Sydney, a quarter to the Society for the Prevention of Cruelty to Animals, and the remainder to a good friend Trevor Mace – engineer and orchardist.

More than a year after her death several beneficiaries co-ordinated a clarification challenge to aspects of the will. Specifically, the neighbouring Adams sisters along with Maude's brother-in-law Ernest Wright challenged the donation of Maude's books going back to where she taught in Sydney at the Ladies College. The outcome of the lawsuit is not known.

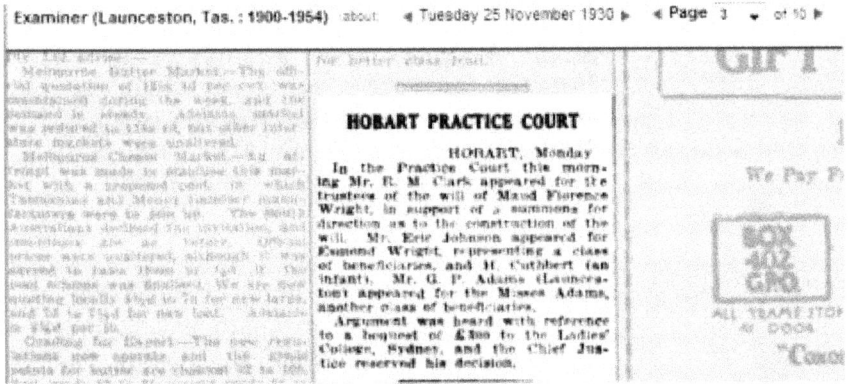

HOBART PRACTICE COURT
IHOBARIT, Monday
In, the Practice Court this morn
Ing Mr. R. M. Clark appeared for the
trustees of the will of Maud Florence
Wright, in support of a summons for
direction as to the construction of the
will. Mr. Eric Johnson appeared for
Esmond Wright, representing a class
of beneficiaries, and H. Cuthbert (an
infant). Mr. G. P. Adams (Launces
ton) appeared for the Misses Adams,
another class of benefielaries.
Argument was heard with reference
to a bequest of £300 to the Ladies'
College, Sydney, and the Chief Jus
tice reserved -his decision.

Author's Relationship to the Wright family

It's a tenuous link between the author and subjects herein. Specifically, the author is related to Maude Rogers who married Howard Wright.

Rogers - > Taylor

Maude was the daughter of Eliza (Taylor) and Edward Rogers (Maude's birth certificate available, parents' marriage certificate available).
Maude married Howard Edward Wright 24 Oct 1888 in Hobart (marriage certificate available).
Eliza is the sister of Joseph Taylor. No direct proof of the brother/sister relationship is available since no birth certificates exist (both born in the UK around 1818/1822). Death certificates of both indicate the same names for mother and father and there is certainly evidence in Eliza's 1872 diary (see the first reference under 'Books' on p62) that she and Joseph were in touch but no known reference indicating he is a brother.

Taylor - > Dent

Joseph Taylor had a son Paul Taylor (birth Certificate available)
Paul Taylor had a daughter Elizabeth Mary Taylor (birth certificate available)
Elizabeth Taylor married Thomas Alfred Dent (marriage certificate available)
They had a son Ronald Thomas Dent (birth certificate available)
Ronald Thomas Dent had a son Warren Dent (birth certificate available)

Author's note: There is no question that the Wrights were a remarkable family. Their business skills, entrepreneurial spirit, risk taking willingness, innate leadership, and human empathy brought them financial rewards, pioneering recognition, and social standing that had them mingling with the rich, famous and influential.

In general they were gracious people, albeit with competitive blood. They exemplified citizens with good taste and good will. They helped establish schools and churches, entertainment and sports centres, provided employment for hundreds, and served as councillors, mayors and founding contributors to social growth and prosperity in the communities they lived in.

Even the extended family practiced the core Wright principles. Maude Rogers, who joined the family, led many charitable causes and opened her house to wounded soldiers requiring extensive rehabilitation. The Wrights were genuine, unselfish, caring souls with highly commendable values, skills and capabilities. All of us who have eaten an apple have unknowingly benefitted from innovation instigated and practiced by the Wrights.

The Wrights of Glenorchy were true pioneers who have left a monumental mark especially in South Australia and Tasmania. We salute them for their contributions to industry and society.

Some Unanswered Questions

Wrights

1. Why did the first Wright sons decide to go to Adelaide?

2. Why did Katherine (Chapman) Wright die so young (age 45). Childbirth? Other?

3. When was Bernard born?

4. Did Ernest and Kate have any children?

5. What happened at The Grove between 1925 and 1940?

6. Why did no Wright relatives want to own and manage The Grove after Kate's death in 1949?

7. How did Howard and Maude meet?

8. What was the contest of Maude's will about and what was its resolution?

9. When was the fountain, now at Quamby, removed from Holebrook Place, and from which property?

References

Books

"Free Settlers and Convicts in Early Australia. A Short History of the Dents and the Taylors 1663 – 2010", by Warren Dent, Infinity Publishing, 2010

"Glenorchy 1804-1964", Alison Alexander. Glenorchy City Council, Glenorchy, Tasmania

Internet Links

Australia Passenger Lists: http://www.blaxland.com/ozships/index.htm

Australian Cemeteries: http://www.coraweb.com.au/cemetaus.htm

Australian Dictionary of Biography: http://adbonline.anu.edu.au/adbonline.htm

Australian Pictures: www.pictureaustralia.org

British Origins Network: http://www.originsnetwork.com/Login2.aspx

Church of Latter Day Saints International Genealogical Index Family Search: http://www.familysearch.org/ENG/search/frameset_search.asp

Deaths Australia - Ryerson Index: http://www.ryersonindex.org

Geanet Online Family Trees : http://gw0.geneanet.org/index.php3?b=alivornesi&lang=en&m=AM&v=8

Henry Hobhouse Turton: http://www.theshipslist.com/accounts/turton.htm

Lambeth Images: http://landmark.lambeth.gov.uk/default.asp

National Library of Australia – find people: http://www.nla.gov.au/find/people.html

Ships in Australia: http://www.flotilla-australia.com/tasother.htm

Trove – search engine of the National Library of Australia: http://trove.nla.gov.au/

Permissions

1. The National Gallery of Australia has given permission to reproduce the image on p12, item www.artsearch.nga.gov.au/Detail.cfm?IRN=143355

2. State Library of Victoria
Coorong Steamship p25. http://www.flotilla-australia.com/images/coorong-slv-b43752.jpg and http://digital.slv.vic.gov.au/view/action/nmets.do?DOCCHOICE=169085.xml&dvs=1298299830904~829&locale=en_US&search_terms=&adjacency=&usePid1=true&usePid2=true. The State Library of Victoria has provided free access to this work to support creativity, innovation and knowledge-exchange. Image H91.325/473 Coorong, by Allan C. Green

3. State Library of South Australia has given permission to reproduce the 5 images on pp 11, 12, 12, 22, 23

PERMISSION GRANTED

I am pleased to grant permission to publish subject to acknowledgement of the State Library of South Australia. The following form of acknowledgement should be used:

Image courtesy of the State Library of South Australia.
SLSA: B 510 British Hotel, Port Adelaide, ca.1880
SLSA: B 1942 Christ Church, North Adelaide, ca.1870
SLSA: B 6586 North Adelaide, ca.1851
SLSA: B 22103/42 Adelaide Book Society: S.P.H. Wright, ca.1880
SLSA: B 60126 Port Adelaide, 1845

It is critical that the images' unique numbers, for example **B 510**, are included as it is the only way we, and any future viewers, can be certain to accurately identify the images.

Permission is for this use only. Any further use requires a separate application.

If you have any further questions regarding this permission to publish application, please let me know. My contact details are: Tel: (08) 82077240; Fax: (08) 82077247; Email: McDonald.Prue@slsa.sa.gov.au

Yours sincerely,

Prue McDonald

Prue McDonald
Research Team
State Library of South Australia

4. State Library of Tasmania. As source of the following images the Tasmanian Archive and Heritage Office has given permission to reproduce:
http://catalogue.statelibrary.tas.gov.au/item/?id=NS738-1-2758 Mr. Harold Wright photo, p35
http://catalogue.statelibrary.tas.gov.au/item/?id=NS738-1-2777 Mrs. Harold Wright photo, p35
http://catalogue.statelibrary.tas.gov.au/item/?id=NS738-1-2804 Mr. Howard Wright photo, p35
http://catalogue.statelibrary.tas.gov.au/item/?id=NS738-1-2729 Mrs. Howard Wright photo, p35
http://catalogue.statelibrary.tas.gov.au/item/?id=NS738-1-2617 Miss Lucy Wayn photo, p46
http://catalogue.statelibrary.tas.gov.au/item/?id=NS738-1-336   Mrs. V. Butler photo, p49

5. Lambeth Archives. Permission granted to publish the following two items on pp 10 and 11
http://landmark.lambeth.gov.uk/display_page.asp?section=landmark&id=11146
http://landmark.lambeth.gov.uk/display_page.asp?section=landmark&id=11101

6. State Library of New South Wales

Derwent (Merchant Steamship) p25.   http://www.flotilla-australia.com/images/derwent-slnsw.jpg
http://acms.sl.nsw.gov.au/item/itemDetailPaged.aspx?itemID=448748   Original held in the Mitchell Library, State Library of NSW, call number: PXE 722 / 1193, digital order number: a637188. Any inquiries about the image, such as requests for copies, should be referred to the Mitchell Library

7. Glenorchy City Council

Use of the photographs of the 'Grove Hop Kiln', 'Hop pickers at the Grove', 'Main Road, Glenorchy' and the 'Poplar Avenue at the Grove' on pp 28, 29, 32 and 34 has been approved by the Heritage Officer and Archivist for Glenorchy City Council. Permission also covers the photo on p30 and the map on p27 which are taken from pages 12 and 20 respectively of Alison Alexander's book "Glenorchy 1804-1964", Glenorchy City Council.

Timeline

The following table shows major events captured in the book by date and lineage. Lineage changes at marriage to the male spouse family name.

Year	Lineage	Event	Location
1730	Tomkins	William born	
1742	Wright	Stephen born, London	
1746	Dixon	Louisa born	
1759	Tomkins	Peltro William chr 15 Oct	
1770	Wilson	John chr. 19 Aug at Canongate, Edinburgh	Chapter 1
1780	Wilson	Andrew born 16 Jan at Canongate, Edinburgh	Chapter 1
1786	Gretton	William Walter born 7 Apr at Whitehall, London, chr 2 May St. Martin in the Fields, Middlesex	Chapter 1
1789	Wright	Stephen Amand chr 26 Apr St. Martin in the Fields, London	Chapter 1
	Tomkins	Lucy Elizabeth born	Chapter 1
1792	Tomkins	William died aged 62	
1797	Wright	Stephen died aged 55	
1807	Wilson/Ker	Andrew married Rachel Ker 21 Oct at Canongate Kirk, Edinburgh	
1809	Wright	Louisa (Dixon) Wright died aged 63	
1816	Gretton/Wright	William married Mary Ann Wright 28 Nov at St. Mary, Lambeth	Chapter 1
1818	Wright/Tomkins	Stephen Amand marries Lucy Elizabeth Tomkins 14 Dec St. George Hanover Sq. London	Chapter 1
1819	Wright	Stephen Peltro Henry chr 2 Dec St. Mary, Lambeth	Chapter 1
1822	Wright	Edward Amand chr 27 Oct at St. Mary, Lambeth	Chapter 1
1824	Wright	Edmund William born 4 Apr at Fulham, London	Chapter 1
1831	Wright	Frederick born 9 Apr, chr 20 May at All saints, Wandsworth	Chapter 1
1839	Gretton/Norton	William married Sarah 28 May at Brussels, Belgium	
1840	Tomkins	Peltro William died 22 Apr Osnaburgh St., London aged 81	
1845	Wright/Howard	Stephen Peltro henry married Elizabeth Jane Howard 12 Sep	Chapter 1
1848	Wilson	Andrew died aged 68	
	Gretton	William died Oct in Bonn, Germany aged 62	
1849	Wright	Howard Edward born Oct in Putney to Stephen and Elizabeth	Chapter 1
1850	Wright	January 17 Stephen, Lucy and daughters Lucy and Amelia leave London for Adelaide	Chapter 1
		June 11 Stephen, Lucy and daughters Lucy and Amelia arrive in Adelaide	Chapter 1
	Chapman	Katherine Maria born in Sunnyside, Hobart	Chapter 2
1851	Wright	Stephen and Lucy build their home "The Gums" in West Torrens	Chapter 1
	Wright	Harold Stephen Robert born 21 Sep to Stephen and Elizabeth in Putney	Chapter 1
1852	Wright/Rippingville	Edmund married Agnes 23 Oct. Agnes was previously married to Henry Stuckey	Chapter 1
1853	Wright/Windsor	Edward married Lucy Ann Windsor 19 Mar in Hobart	Chapter 1
1854	Wright	Ernest Charles was born April in Putney to Stephen and Elizabeth	Chapter 1
1855	Wright	Lucy Elizabeth (Tomkins) died 12 Sep at Lockleys, Adelaide, South Australia aged 66	Chapter 1
1860	Wright	Stephen Amand died 2 Mar in Paris aged 71	Chapter 1
1861	Rogers	Maude Florence born 27 Aug in Sydney to Edward and Eliza	Chapter 2
1866	Wright	Stephen Peltro Henry moved his family to Glenorchy in January	Chapter 1
1874	Wright/O'Halloran	Mona Jane married Henry Dunkin O'Halloran 5 August	Chapter 2

1882	Wright/Bisdee	Eva Dorinda married Winchester Dunn At St. Paul's Glenorchy 16 January	Chapter 2
1884	Wright	Elizabeth Jane (Howard) died 13 April at The Grove aged 64	Chapter 2
	Wright	Harold Stephen Robert married Katherine Maria Chapman 1 October in Hobart	Chapter 2
1885	Wright	Esmond Stephen Kennard born 20 Sep to Harold and Katherine	Chapter 2
1886	Wright	Stephen Peltro Henry died 15 Sep aged 65 at The Grove, Glenorchy, Tasmania	Chapter 2
1888	Wright	Edmund William died 5 Aug at North Adelaide aged 64	Chapter 2
	Wright/Rogers	Howard Edward married Maude Florence 24 October in Hobart	Chapter 2
1889	Wright/Butler	Ernest Charles married Kate Amelia 8 June at All Saints Church, Glenorchy	Chapter 2
1890	Wright	Kate Ione Howard born 14 Jun to Harold and Katherine	Chapter 2
1891	Wright	Edward Amand died 13 Jun aged 69	Chapter 2
1895	Wright	Katherine Maria (Chapman) died 8 December at The Grove	Chapter 2
1898	Wright/Thorne	Nora Elizabeth married Arthur Edward Thorne at St. Pauls' Glenorchy 23 March	Chapter 2
1902	Wright/Wayn	Harold married Mary Louisa 5 Dec at ST. John's Toorak, Victoria	Chapter 2
1910	Wright	Bernard died Aug 20 at Jericho	Chapter 2
1924	Wright	Howard Edward died 6 Sep in Hobart	Chapter 2
1925	Wright	Ernest died in April	Chapter 2
1929	Wright	Maude Florence (Rogers) died 27 July in Hobart	Chapter 2
1932	Wright	Mary Louisa (Wayn) died 16 Dec in Hobart	Chapter 2
1933	Wright/Longmore	Esmond married Ethel 4 Mar in Hobart	Chapter 2
1940	Wright	Harold leaves the Grove to live with Esmond and Ethel in Sandy Bay	Chapter 2
1942	Wright	Harold Stephen Robert dies 4 Jan at a Private Hospital, Hobart	Chapter 2
1949	Wright	Kate Ione died and estate put up for sale	Chapter 2
1950	Estate	B. Mollineaux, buys Estate now down to 8 acres	Chapter 2
1952	Estate	Remnants are sold off	Chapter 2

Footnotes:

Chapter 1

1. http://books.google.com/books?id=n4EwAAAAIAAJ&pg=PA369&lpg=PA369&dq=%22stephen+amand+wright%22&source=bl&ots=vwJx0sm6mf&sig=E1n3E_RBMESHfnIk9gvcV-xZszI&hl=en&ei=CmrITOnrJoL0tgPyj-GwCw&sa=X&oi=book_result&ct=result&resnum=9&ved=0CEUQ6AEwCA#v=onepage&q=%22stephen%20amand%20wright%22&f=false

   > after Michaelmas term, 1846, it appeared that, in November 1842, an agreement was executed between William Walker Gretton, Stephen Amand Wright, and John Wilson, trustees under the will of John Gretton, of the first part, Emma Haffner, the cestui que trust, of the second part, William Belton of the third part, and Peter Belton of the fourth part; whereby, after reciting that William Belton was already assignee of a term of thirty years from Michaelmas 1814 in the after-mentioned houses and premises, situate in the Mile End Road, in the parish of St. Dunstan, Stepney, and that the parties of the first part, with the consent of Emma Haffner, had acceded to W. Belton's request that they should grant him a lease as after mentioned, it was witnessed that W. Belton

2. http://www.mit.edu/~dfm/genealogy/gretton.html#
   William Walter GRETTON, b. 7 Apr 1786 at Whitehall, London, chr. 2 May 1786 at St. Martin in the Fields, Middlesex, m1. 28 Nov 1816 at St. Mary, Lambeth, Mary Ann WRIGHT, m2. 28 May 1839 at Brussels, Belgium, Sarah NORTON (b. 30 Oct 1816 at Broadstairs or St. Peters, Kent, d. 25 Oct 1887, d. reg. Q4 1887 at Pancras R.D., bur. at Brompton Cemetery), d. Oct 1848 at Bonn, Germany, bur. at Bonn. Educated at Magdalene College, Cambridge University (admitted pensioner 30 Jan 1801, matriculated Michaelmas 1801, scholar, B.A. 1806, M.A. 1809). At his marriage in 1816, of The Lodge, South Lambeth. At his son's baptism in 1819, a gentleman, of South Lambeth. At his son's baptism in 1822, "esquire", of South Lambeth. Called to the bar, Lincoln's Inn, 10 Feb 1824. At his son's baptism in Dec 1824, a barrister at law, of South Lambeth. At his son's admission to St. Paul's School in 1828, a barrister, of Lodge, South Lambeth. When his will was proved in the Prerogative Court of Canterbury on 5 May 1849, a barrister at law, of Bonn. At the announcement of his son's marriage in 1850, formerly of Westcote Hall, Leicestershire. In 1881, Sarah was a house owner, living at 36 Princess Terrace, London, with her daughter Augusta and a German servant.

3.
   IGI Individual Record
   Search Results | Download | Print

   FamilySearch™ International Genealogical Index v5.0
   British Isles

   Stephen Wright
   Male
   Pedigree

   Event(s):
   Birth: About 1742 Springgardens, Stmartininfields, , London, England
   Christening:
   Death: 1797
   Burial:

   Messages:
   Record submitted after 1991 by a member of the LDS Church. No additional information is available. Ancestral File may list the same family and the submitter.

   Source Information:
   No source information is available.

IGI Individual Record

FamilySearch™ International Genealogical Index v5.0
British Isles

Search Results | Download | Print

Louisa Dixon   Pedigree
Female

Event(s):
Birth: About 1746 , , England
Christening:
Death: 1809
Burial:

Messages:
Record submitted after 1991 by a member of the LDS Church. No additional information is available. Ancestral File may list the same family and the submitter.

Source Information:
No source information is available.

Proof of marriage: http://www.florin.ms/cemetery3.html

*§ AMELIA AUGUSTA LE MESURIER/ ENGLAND / Mesurier (Le)/ Amalia Augusta / / Inghilterra/ Firenze/ 7 Febbraio/ 1845/ Anni 48/ 304/ GI.23774 N° 74 Burial 09/02, Rev Robbins; Marriage 29/09/23 Edward Le Mesurier to Amelia Augusta Wright at BCL, groom aged 28 s of Havilland Le Mesurier and Elisabeth Dobree of Guernsey, bride age 27 from Middlesex. d of Stephen Wright and Louisa Dixon, in Genoa, see Webb for further details. (Rounded slab) SACRED/ TO THE MEMORY OF/ AMELIA AUGUSTA/ THE BELOVED WIFE OF/ EDWARD LE MESURIER ESQ R.N./ WHO DEPARTED THIS LIFE IN FLORENCE/ FEBRUARY THE 7TH 1845 AGED 48/ HER CHILDREN ARISE UP AND CALL HER/ BLESSED HER HUSBAND ALSO AND HE/ PRAISETH HER/ BLESSED ARE THE DEAD WHICH DIE IN THE LORD EVEN SO SAITH THE SPIRIT/ FOR THEY REST FROM THEIR LABOURS/ A3N(35)

4. http://books.google.com/books?id=6SI8AAAAIAAJ&pg=PA548&dq=wilson#v=onepage&q=wilson&f=false

WILSON, ANDREW (1780–1848), landscape-painter, born in Edinburgh in 1780, came of an old family who had suffered in the Jacobite cause. His father's name was Archibald Wilson, his mother's Elizabeth Shields. When quite young he commenced to study art under Alexander Nasmyth [q. v.], and then, at the age of seventeen, went to London, where he worked for some time in the schools of the Royal Academy. Proceeding to Italy, he studied the great works of the Italian masters, thus laying the foundation of a knowledge which afterwards proved of great use, and he became acquainted with the well-known collectors Champernown and Irving. He also made many sketches, principally of the architecture in the neighbourhood of Rome and Naples. Returning to London in 1803, he at once saw the advantage of importing pictures by the old masters, and went back to Italy for that purpose. The troubled state of Europe made travelling difficult, but he reached Genoa, where he settled under the protection of the American consul and was elected a member of the Ligurian Academy. As a member of that society he was present when Napoleon Bonaparte visited its exhibition, and on some envious academician informing the latter, who had paused to admire Wilson's picture, that it was by an Englishman, he was met by the retort: 'Le talent n'a pas de pays.' In 1805 he returned through Germany to London with the pictures (over fifty in number) which he had acquired. Among them were Rubens's 'Brazen Serpent' (now in the National Gallery) and Bassano's 'Adoration of the Magi' (in the Edinburgh Gallery).

Settling in London, he painted a good deal in watercolour, was one of the original members of the Associated Artists (1808), and held for a period the position of teacher of drawing in Sandhurst Military College; but being in 1818 appointed master of the Trustees' Academy, he removed to Edinburgh, where he exercised a considerable and beneficial influence upon his pupils, among whom were Robert Scott Lauder [q. v.], William Simson [q. v.], and David Octavius Hill [q. v.] While in London he contributed to the Royal Academy, and in Edinburgh he supported the Royal Institution, of which he was the manager as well as an artist associate member. But his predilection for Italy was too strong to be resisted, and in 1826, taking his wife and family with him, he again went south, and for the twenty years following lived in Rome, Florence, and Genoa. During this period he was much consulted on art matters, collected pictures for Lords Hopetoun and Pembroke, Sir Robert Peel, and others, and was instrumental in securing for the Royal Institution some of the most important works, which later helped to form the

National Gallery of Scotland. He also painted much in both oil and watercolours, and his work, some of the finest of which never came to this country, was in great request by artistic visitors to Italy. His pictures are delicate in handling, refined in colour, pleasant in composition, and serene in effect. He is represented in the Scottish National Gallery by two Italian landscapes and a 'View of Burntisland' in oils, and by three watercolours in the watercolour collection at South Kensington. In 1847, leaving his family in Italy, he revisited Scotland, but, on the eve of returning, he died in Edinburgh on 27 Nov. 1848.

In 1808 he married Rachel Ker, daughter of William Ker, descendant of the Inglis of Manner, and had a family of four sons and three daughters. The eldest son, Charles Heath Wilson, is separately noticed.

[Edinburgh Annual Register, 1816; Catalogue of the Exhibition of Works by Scottish Artists, Edinburgh, 1863; Redgrave's and Bryan's Dictionaries; Armstrong's Scottish Painters, 1888; Brydall's Art in Scotland, 1889; Catalogues of Royal Institution, Edinburgh, Royal Academy, Scottish National Gallery, South Kensington; information from C. A. Wilson, esq., Genoa.]　　　　　　　　　　J. L. C.

IGI Individual Record

FamilySearch™ International Genealogical Index v5.0

British Isles

Search Results | Download | Print

Andrew Wilson　　　　　　　　　　　　　　　　　　　　　　　Pedigree
Male

Event(s):
Birth:　　　　16 JAN 1780　Cannongate, Edinb, , Midlothian, Scotland
Christening:
Death:
Burial:

Parents:
Father:　　　Thomas Wilson　　　　　　　　　　　　　　　　　　　Family
Mother:　　　Elizabeth Burt

Messages:
Record submitted by a member of the LDS Church. The record often shows the name of the individual and his or her relationship to a descendant, shown as the heir, family representative, or relative. The original records are not indexed, and you may have to look at the film frame-by-frame to find the information you want. A family group record for this couple may be in the Family Group Record Collection; Archive Section. (See the Family History Library Catalog for the film number.) These records are alphabetical by name of the father or husband.

Source Information:
Film Number:　　446014
Page Number:
Reference number: 51063

IGI Individual Record

FamilySearch™ International Genealogical Index v5.0
British Isles

Search Results | Download | Print

JOHN WILLSON
Male

Pedigree

Event(s):
Birth:
Christening: 19 AUG 1770 Canongate, Edinburgh, Midlothian, Scotland
Death:
Burial:

Parents:
Father: THOMAS WILLSON
Mother: ELIZABETH BAIRT

Family

Messages:
Extracted birth or christening record for the locality listed in the record. The source records are usually arranged chronologically by the birth or christening date.

Source Information:
Batch No.:	Dates:	Source Call No.:	Type:	Printout Call No.:	Type:
C119997	1756 - 1795	1067742	Film	6900995	Film
Sheet:					

'Proof' that John and Andrew were brothers (although Will(l)son is misspelled and two versions of mother's maiden name are shown

5.

IGI Individual Record

FamilySearch™ International Genealogical Index v5.0
British Isles

Search Results | Download | Print

STEPHEN AMAND WRIGHT
Male

Pedigree

Event(s):
Birth:
Christening: 26 APR 1789 Saint Martin In The Fields, Westminster, London, England
Death:
Burial:

Parents:
Father: STEPHEN WRIGHT
Mother: LOUISA

Family

Messages:
Extracted birth or christening record for the locality listed in the record. The source records are usually arranged chronologically by the birth or christening date.

Source Information:
Batch No.:	Dates:	Source Call No.:	Type:	Printout Call No.:	Type:
C001459	1775 - 1797	0561144	Film	6901249	Film
Sheet: 00					

http://books.google.com/books?id=0wXkAAAAMAAJ&pg=PA593&lpg=PA593&dq=%22Stephen+Amand+Wright%22&source=bl&ots=1MiaJL-qo9&sig=w1JtICfI4pfFA2ZVJs5inNZ62-c&hl=en&ei=U9ILTZX3E4y4sAO9vsmTCg&sa=X&oi=book_result&ct=result&resnum=1&ved=0CBkQ6AEwAA#v=onepage&q=%22Stephen%20Amand%20Wright%22&f=false

Lineage.

STEPHEN WRIGHT, of Spring Gardens, in the parish of St. Martin-in-the-Fields, and of Hammersmith, co. Middlesex, m. Louisa DIXON (who d. 1809), and d. 1797, having had issue,
 1. STEPHEN AMAND, of whom presently.
 1. Charlotte, m. James STOW.
 11. Mary, m. William Walter GRETTON.
 111. Eliza, m. Alexander CARSON.
 1V. Louisa.
 V. Caroline, m.
 V1. Amelia, m. Edward LE MESURIER.

The only son,
STEPHEN AMAND WRIGHT, m. 1793, Miss TOMKINS (who d. 1854), and d. 1857, having had issue,
 1. STEPHEN PELTRO HENRY, of whom presently.
 11. Edward Amand, m. Lucy WINDSOR.
 111. Edmund W., m. Agnes STUCKEY.
 1V. Arthur James, m. Isabel WINDSOR.
 V. Frederick, m. Frances Jane, daughter of Major Thomas Shuldham O'HALLORAN, of Lizard Lodge, South Australia (see that family).

 1V. Nora Elizabeth.
 1. Lucy, m. Peter D. PRANKERD.
 11. Amelia, m. Richard HICKS.

The eldest son,
STEPHEN PELTRO HENRY WRIGHT, b. 1819; m. at the parish church of King Curran, near Kinsale, co. Cork, Ireland, 12th September, 1845, Elizabeth Jane HOWARD (who d. 13th April, 1884), and d. 15th September, 1886, having had issue,
 1. Howard Edward, m. October, 1888, Maude Florence ROGERS, but has no issue.
 11. HAROLD STEPHEN ROBERT, of Glenorchy, the subject of this memoir.
 111. Ernest Charles, m. June, 1889, Katherine Amelia BUTLER, but has no issue.
 1V. Bernard Howard.
 1. Marian Lucy.
 11. Mona Jane, m. 5th August, 1874, Henry Dunkin O'HALLORAN, but has no issue (see that family).
 111. Eva Dorinda, m. 16th January, 1883, Winchester Munn BISDEE, and has issue, three sons and one daughter.

Arms—Or a fesse chequy arg. and az. between three eagles' heads erased of the third langued gu.
Crest—A unicorn passant reguardant quarterly arg. and az. armed and crined or.
Motto—Mens conscia recti.
Residence—The Grove, Glenorchy, near Hobart, Tasmania.
Club—Tasmanian, in Hobart.

VOL. II. 2 Q

http://www.mit.edu/~dfm/genealogy/gretton.html#Wright

Wright

Stephen WRIGHT, m. Louisa. Of Stockwell, Surrey. [ref 3y,5e]

1. Charlotte Hannah WRIGHT, chr. 10 Jun 1781 at St. Martin in the Fields, Middlesex. [ref 3t]
2. Stephen George WRIGHT, chr. 27 Oct 1782 at St. Martin in the Fields. [ref 3t]
3. Harriot Elizabeth WRIGHT, chr. 11 Sep 1785 at St. Martin in the Fields. [ref 3t]
4. Mary Ann WRIGHT, chr. Aug 1787 at St. Martin in the Fields, m. 28 Nov 1816 at St. Mary, Lambeth, Surrey, William Walter GRETTON, d. 9 Nov 1834, bur. at Milton by Gravesend, Kent. At her marriage in 1816, of Stockwell Place, Surrey. [ref 3h,3t,4h,5e]
5. Stephen Amand WRIGHT, chr. 26 Apr 1789 at St. Martin in the Fields, m. 14 Dec 1818 at St. George Hanover Square, Middlesex, Lucy Elizabeth TOMKINS (eldest daughter of Peltro William TOMKINS, an engraver and print publisher in New Bond Street [see Dictionary of National Biography and works in the National Portrait Gallery]). At his marriage in 1818, of Stockwell Place, Surrey, and the parish of St. Mary, Lambeth; Lucy was of the parish of St. George Hanover Square; the witnesses were Peltro William TOMKINS (Lucy's father) and Francis P. TOMKINS (perhaps a brother or an uncle). At his son's baptism in 1819, a gentleman, of Stockwell. At his daughter's baptism in 1821, of Clapham. At his son's baptism in 1822, a gentleman, of Brixton. At his son's baptism in 1831, "esquire", of Wandsworth, Surrey. In the 1843 Post Office Directory, a senior clerk in the Store Account Examiner's Office of the Ordnance Board, at the Tower of London. [ref 3h,3t,3w,3y,3z,4t,10a]
   1. Stephen Peltro Henry WRIGHT, b. ca. 1819 at Stockwell, chr. 2 Dec 1819 at St. Mary, Lambeth, m. Elizabeth Jane HOWARD (b. ca. 1819 at Kensale, Co. Cork). At his children's baptisms in 1848 and 1849, a gentleman, of Putney, Surrey. In Mar 1851, a clerk in the Ordnance Department at the Tower, living in High Street, Putney, with his wife Elizabeth, their children Marian, Mona, and Howard, his wife's widowed mother Mary Ann (a landed proprietor, b. ca. 1791 at Bandow, Co. Cork), Jane WARREN (a fund holder, relationship not stated, b. ca. 1775 at Kensington, Middlesex), and three servants. At his sons' baptisms in Oct 1851 and 1854, a gentleman, of Putney. [ref 2b,3t,5s]
      1. Marian WRIGHT, b. ca. 1846 at Wandsworth, Surrey. In 1851, living with her parents. [ref 2b]
      2. Mona Jane WRIGHT, b. ca. 1847 at Putney, chr. 5 Jan 1848 at St. Mary, Putney. In 1851, living with her parents. [ref 2b,3s]
      3. Howard Edward WRIGHT, b. ca. Oct 1849 at Putney, chr. 14 Nov 1849 at St. Mary, Putney. In 1851, living with his parents [ref 2b,3s]
      4. Harrold Stephen Robert WRIGHT, chr. 15 Oct 1851 at St. Mary, Putney. [ref 3s]
      5. Ernest Charles WRIGHT, chr. 11 Jan 1854 at St. Mary, Putney. [ref 3s]
   2. Lucy Amelia WRIGHT, b. 22 Mar 1821, chr. 30 Mar 1821 at Clapham, Surrey. [ref 3y]
   3. Edward Amand WRIGHT, chr. 27 Oct 1822 at St. Mary, Lambeth. [ref 3h]
   4. Frederick WRIGHT, b. 9 Apr 1831, chr. 20 May 1831 at All Saints, Wandsworth. [ref 3w]
6. Elizabeth Ann WRIGHT, chr. 13 Mar 1791 at St. Martin in the Fields. [ref 3t]
7. Louisa Harriot WRIGHT, chr. 8 Jul 1792 at St. Martin in the Fields. [ref 3t]
8. Caroline Augusta WRIGHT, chr. 9 Nov 1794 at St. Martin in the Fields. [ref 3t]
9. Amelia Augusta WRIGHT, chr. 31 Oct 1796 at St. Martin in the Fields and apparently also in 1796 at St. Paul, Hammersmith, Middlesex, m. 1822 Edward LE MESURIER, d. 1845. [ref 3t,3v,5a,5e]

6.

The register book of marriages belonging to the parish of St ..., Volume 3 By Westminster, England. St. George, Hanover square (Parish)

ST. GEORGE, HANOVER SQUARE. 171

1818
Nov. 28 Charles Burrough Strong, of S⁺ Pancras, B., & Jane Winter Gray, S., of this parish. Licence
Nov. 29 Thomas Tyer, W., of Putney, & Mary Perch, S., of this parish. Licence
Nov. 29 Maurice de Vigmon, W., & Gustavin de Pruili, S. Licence
Nov. 29 John Milsted & Mary Peacock
Nov. 29 Thomas Pratt & Mary Aldham
Nov. 29 Joseph Eavry & Mary Toole
Nov. 29 Dennis Carthy & Margaret Collins
Dec. 1 William Taylor & Margaret Carey
Dec. 1 Joseph Burgis & Kitty Putman
Dec. 2 George Penn & Elizabeth Buttle
Dec. 3 Thomas Muggeridge, of this parish, B., & Anne Andrus, of Ashinthe, co. Kent, S. Licence
Dec. 4 William Lumley Fifield & Temperance Sanders
Dec. 5 Saint John Bygrave, B., of this parish, & Mary North Chadwell, S., of S⁺ Mary Abbotts, Kensington. Licence
Dec. 5 George Hornby & Agnes Rowan
Dec. 5 James Gilbert & Elizabeth Sargeant
Dec. 5 Thomas Shorter & Hannah Jeyes
Dec. 6 James Carter & Cordelia Hester Herbert
Dec. 6 William Backshell & Hannah Graham
Dec. 6 Richard Reeve & Mary Underrise
Dec. 6 John Jelley & Mary Ann Long
Dec. 6 James Connell & Emma Richards
Dec. 6 John Brown & Mary Sanders
Dec. 8 Edward Barker & Rachel Preslidge
Dec. 8 Alexander Allen Jackson & Ann Berry
Dec. 9 James Lawrence & Frances Dyer
Dec. 9 George Mann & Esther Jones
Dec. 9 Richard Buttock, of Sunning, co. Oxford, W., & Sarah Sharp, S. Licence
Dec. 9 John Whish, B., & Julia Stokes, S.
Dec. 11 Robert Summers & Sarah Radley
Dec. 13 Joseph Sear & Abigial Granger
Dec. 13 George Cock Parke & Mary Ann Rowlands
Dec. 14 John Dell & Charlotte Eaton
Dec. 14 Charles Fenn & Mary Ann Fenn
Dec. 14 William Child & Elizabeth Kirkman
Dec. 14 George Mackenzie & Elizabeth Dean
Dec. 14 Stephen Amand Wright, B., of S⁺ Mary, Lambeth, Surry, & Lucy Elizabeth Tomkins, of this parish, S. Licence
Dec. 14 William Clifford Smith & Mary Smith
Dec. 14 William Tubbs & Hannah Lankester
Dec. 14 Richard Warner & Esher Richardson
Dec. 14 William Conquest & Mary Conquest

7. See note 5 above plus

IGI Individual Record FamilySearch™ International Genealogical Index v5.0
British Isles

Search Results | Download | Print

PELTRO WILLIAM TOMKINS — Pedigree
Male — Family

Event(s):
Birth:
Christening:
Death:
Burial:

Marriages:
Spouse: LUCY JONES — Family
Marriage: 02 JUN 1787 Saint Clement Danes, Westminster, London, England

Messages:
Extracted marriage record for locality listed in the record. The source records are usually arranged chronologically by the marriage date.

Source Information:

Batch No.	Dates	Source Call No.	Type	Printout Call No.	Type
M041601	1754 - 1777	0574460	Film	6903795	Film
M041601	1777 - 1802	0574461	Film	NONE	
M041601	1802 - 1837	0574462	Film	NONE	
M041601	1837 - 1860	0574463	Film	NONE	
M041601	1860 - 1875	0574464	Film	NONE	
M041601	1876 - 1885	0574465	Film	6903795	Film

Sheet: 00

http://books.google.com/books?id=xicJAAAAIAAJ&pg=PA8&dq=%22Tomkins,+Peltro+William%22&hl=en&ei=oNULTaPLF5L4sAO2osnWCg&sa=X&oi=book_result&ct=result&resnum=2&ved=0CCkQ6AEwAQ#v=onepage&q=%22Tomkins%2C%20Peltro%20William%22&f=false

TOMKINS, PELTRO WILLIAM (1759-1840), engraver and draughtsman, was born in London in 1759 (baptised 15 Oct.) He was younger son of WILLIAM TOMKINS (1730?-1792), landscape-painter, by his wife Susanna Callard.

In 1763 the father gained the second premium of the Society of Arts for a landscape, and subsequently, through the patronage of Edward Walter of Stalbridge, obtained considerable employment in painting views, chiefly of scenery in the north and west of England. He imitated the manner of Claude, many of whose works, as well as those of some of the Dutch painters, he also copied. He exhibited with the Free Society of Artists from 1761 to 1764, with the Incorporated Society from 1764 to 1768, and at the Royal Academy annually from 1769 to 1790. He was elected an associate of the academy in 1771. Some of Tomkins's works were engraved in Angus's and Watts's sets of views of seats of the nobility. He died at his house in Queen Anne Street, London, on 1 Jan. 1792.

The younger son, Peltro, became one of the ablest pupils of Francesco Bartolozzi [q.v.], working entirely in the dot and stipple style, and produced many fine plates, of which the most attractive are 'A Dressing Room à l'Anglaise,' and 'A Dressing Room à la Française,' a pair after Charles Ansell; 'English Fireside' and 'French Fireside,' a pair after C. Ansell; 'Cottage Girl shelling Peas' and 'Village Girl gathering Nuts,' a pair after William Redmore Bigg; 'Amyntor and Theodora,' after Thomas Stothard; 'The Vestal,' after Reynolds; 'Sylvia and Daphne,' after Angelica Kauffmann; 'Louisa,' after James Nixon; 'Birth of the Thames,' after Maria Cosway; 'Madonna della Tenda,' after Raphael; portrait of Mrs. Siddons, after John Downman; and portrait of the Duchess of Norfolk, after L. da Heere. He was also largely employed upon the illustrations to Sharpe's 'British Poets,' 'British Classics,' and 'British Theatre.' Tomkins was a clever original artist, and engraved from his own

8. See note 5 above
9. See http://www.mit.edu/~dfm/genealogy/gretton.html#LeMesurier

Le Mesurier

For more, see *Rough Index to the Le Mesurier Family*.

Edward LE MESURIER, b. ca. 1792, m. 1822 Amelia Augusta WRIGHT, d. 1854. Served in the Royal Navy during the Napoleonic Wars. In 1817, a lieutenant on half pay, settled in Genoa as a merchant. [ref 5a]

1. Amelia Louisa Vaux LE MESURIER, b. 28 Dec 1823 at Genoa, m. 19 Oct 1849 at Leghorn, George Mussell GRETTON, d. 30 Mar 1894, d. reg. Q1 1894 at Fulham R.D., bur. at Fulham old cemetery. Author of *The Vicissitudes of Italy Since the Congress of Vienna* (1859) and *The Englishwoman in Italy: Impressions of Life in the Roman States and Sardinia During a Ten Years' Residence* (1860). In 1891, living on her own means with her son George. [ref 1a,2f,4b1,5a,5e]
2. Edward Algernon LE MESURIER, b. 14 Sep 1839 at Ancona, Italy, m. 20 Jul 1865 at St. Mary's Episcopal Chapel, Renfield Street, Glasgow, Elizabeth Agnes WILSON, d. 7 Feb 1903 at Villa Cipressi, Genoa. At his marriage in 1865, a banker, of Genoa. [ref 4d1,5a]
   1. Agnes Augusta LE MESURIER, b. 1878 at Genoa, m. 29 Mar 1906 at Chinsurah, India, John Cunliffe GRETTON. [ref 5a]

10. See note 5 above
11. http://www.lambeth.gov.uk/Services/AboutLambeth/StockwellHistory.htm
12. See note 5 above

13. See note 5 above
14. http://adbonline.anu.edu.au/biogs/AS10500b.htm
15. http://www.architectsdatabase.unisa.edu.au/arch_full.asp?Arch_ID=17
16. http://adbonline.anu.edu.au/biogs/AS10500b.htm
17. See note 5 above and

IGI Individual Record

FamilySearch™ International Genealogical Index v5.0
British Isles

Search Results | Download | Print

STEPHEN PELTRO HENRY WRIGHT Pedigree
Male

Event(s):
Birth:
Christening: 02 DEC 1819 Saint Mary, Lambeth, Surrey, England
Death:
Burial:

Parents:
Father: STEPHEN AMAUD WRIGHT   Family
Mother: ELIZABETH

Messages:
Extracted birth or christening record for locality listed in the record. The source records are usually arranged chronologically by the birth or christening date.

Source Information:

Batch No.:	Dates:	Source Call No.:	Type:	Printout Call No.:	Type:
P006281	1800 - 1822	0254603-0254607	Film	0821156	Film
P006281	1800 - 1822	0254603-0254607	Film	0821157	Film

Sheet: 00

18. See note 5 above and

IGI Individual Record

FamilySearch™ International Genealogical Index v5.0
British Isles

Search Results | Download | Print

STEPHEN PETTRO HENRY WRIGHT Pedigree
Male Family

Event(s):
Birth:
Christening:
Death:
Burial:

Marriages:
Spouse: ELIZABETH JANE HOWARD   Family
Marriage: 12 SEP 1845 All Saints, Wandsworth, London, England
Husband Age at Marriage: 25
Wife Age at Marriage: 24

Messages:
Extracted marriage record for locality listed in the record. The source records are usually arranged chronologically by the marriage date.

Source Information:

Batch No.:	Dates:	Source Call No.:	Type:	Printout Call No.:	Type:
M019011	1603 - 1788	0599302 IT 1	Film	1037030	Film
M019011	1801 - 1822	0307713	Film	NONE	
M019011	1823 - 1842	0307714	Film	NONE	
M019011	1843 - 1854	0307715	Film	NONE	

Sheet: 00

19. See note 5 above

20. See note 5 above and

IGI Individual Record

FamilySearch™ International Genealogical Index v5.0
British Isles

Search Results | Download | Print

Amelia Wright — Pedigree
Female

Event(s):
- Birth: About 1833 Spring Gardens, Stmartininfields, , London, England
- Christening:
- Death:
- Burial:

Parents:
- Father: Stephen Amand Wright — Family
- Mother: Tomkins

Messages:
Record submitted after 1991 by a member of the LDS Church. No additional information is available. Ancestral File may list the same family and the submitter.

Source Information:
No source information is available.

21. http://www.theshipslist.com/ships/australia/fatima1850.htm

  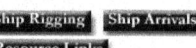

Kindly transcribed and submitted to TheShipsList by Robert Janmaat, Adelaide, from a variety of sources, cited below.
Return to SA Passenger Lists, 1847-1886

barque **Fatima**, 521 tons, Captain George Ray, from London 17th January 1850 / Plymouth 13th February 1850, arrived at Port Adelaide, South Australia 11th June 1850.

South Australian Register Wenesday 12 June 1850

Tuesday June 11- The Barque **Fatima** 521 tons, Ray master, from London 17 Jan., Plymouth 13 Feb.
Passengers: John Wilkins Esq. M.D. Surgeon, Mr. and Mrs. Wright, Miss Lucy Wright, Miss Amelia Wright, Mr. Henry Hobhouse Turton, Mr. and Mrs. Clark and eight children in the cabin.— *5th ship from England to S.A. with government passengers for 1850 ; John Wilkins, surgeon-superintendent ; four births and three deaths on the passage*

22. The account of this voyage was based on a diary kept by the lad Henry Hobhouse Turton (Harry) and published as http://www.theshipslist.com/accounts/turton.htm

23. In 2008 the West Torrens council identified the house as an historic site. See http://www.wtcc.sa.gov.au/webdata/resources/files/060508_Council_and_Committee_Agenda_full_document.pdf

24. See http://www.architectsdatabase.unisa.edu.au/arch_full.asp?Arch_ID=17

25.

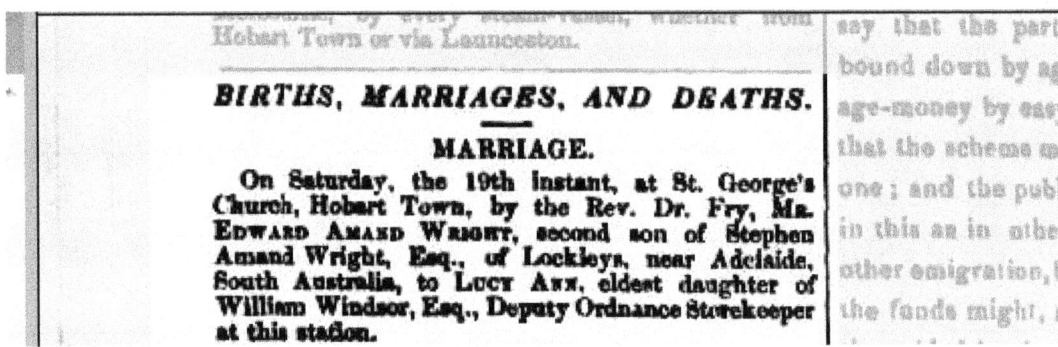

IGI Individual Record

FamilySearch™ International Genealogical Index v5.0
Southwest Pacific

Search Results | Download | Print

EDWARD ARMAND WRIGHT
Male

Pedigree
Family

Event(s):
Birth:
Christening:
Death:
Burial:

Marriages:
Spouse: LUCY ANN WINDSOR
Marriage: 19 MAR 1853 , Tasmania, Australia
Husband Age at Marriage: 31
Wife Age at Marriage: 28

Family

Messages:
Extracted marriage record for locality listed in the record. The source records are usually arranged chronologically by the marriage date.

Source Information:

Batch No.:	Dates:	Source Call No.:	Type:	Printout Call No.:	Type:
M310467	1853 - 1854	1368291	Film	NONE	
Sheet: 00					

26. See

http://familytreemaker.genealogy.com/users/w/i/n/Cidney-Noel-Windsor-Tasmania/WEBSITE-0001/UHP-0250.html
http://familytreemaker.genealogy.com/users/w/i/n/Cidney-Noel-Windsor-Tasmania/WEBSITE-0001/UHP-0227.html

http://familytreemaker.genealogy.com/users/w/i/n/Cidney-Noel-Windsor-Tasmania/WEBSITE-0001/UHP-0225.html
http://familytreemaker.genealogy.com/users/w/i/n/Cidney-Noel-Windsor-Tasmania/WEBSITE-0001/UHP-0219.html
http://familytreemaker.genealogy.com/users/w/i/n/Cidney-Noel-Windsor-Tasmania/WEBSITE-0001/UHP-0217.html
http://familytreemaker.genealogy.com/users/w/i/n/Cidney-Noel-Windsor-Tasmania/WEBSITE-0001/UHP-0206.html
http://familytreemaker.genealogy.com/users/w/i/n/Cidney-Noel-Windsor-Tasmania/WEBSITE-0001/UHP-0031.html

27.

PIONEER DAYS

Mr. H. S. R. Wright's Reminiscences

Prominent Glenorchy resident for many years, Mr. Harold S. R. Wright celebrated his 88th birthday anniversary on Saturday. He lived at the Grove estate, Glenorchy, for 72 years, and was Warden of the municipality for 11 years. In his young days he was a keen oarsman and yachtsman. He left the Grove a few weeks ago and is living with his son, Mr. Esmond Wright, Lower Sandy Bay.

Mr. Wright, who was born in London, travelled to South Australia with his father, Mr. S. P. H. Wright, in 1855. Ten years later the family moved to Tasmania, where the Grove estate was acquired. Mr. Wright completed his education at the Hobart High School, then conducted by Mr. R. D. Poulett-Harris.

Mr. Wright told a representative of "The Mercury" there was friendly controversy between the Shoobridge family and his own as to which shipped overseas the first export cases of Tasmanian apples. The first consignment bearing the Wright brand was sent to England before the days of refrigerated space in ships. Only one case arrived in marketable condition. The price, 7/., satisfied the consignors that a payable trade could be developed. Barrels, imported from America, were next used, and the better ventilation they afforded resulted in the fruit being landed in England in better condition. Mr. Wright remembers a season in which 5,000 cases of apples were picked from 4½ acres on the Grove property. His family claims to having pioneered the practice of apple wrapping. Hops also were grown extensively at the Grove.

Mr. Wright remembers the bushrangers, Martin Cash and Rheuben Priest, in their "respectable" days at Glenorchy. Priest, he said, made a point of being the first resident to pay his rates each year.

A vivid memory is that of a landslip on the shoulder of Mt. Wellington, above Glenorchy, in 1872. It was accompanied by flood damage to the areas below. Thousands of tons of bush timber were deposited on the Grove, and a tree 75ft. long was carried by the rush of water close to the homestead. On higher slopes stones borne by the torrent were left entangled in tree boughs 50ft. above the ground.

PIONEER DAYS

Mr. H. S. R. Wright's Reminiscences

In the course of reminiscences of Mr. H. S. R. Wright published in "The Mercury" on Tuesday last, it was stated that Mr. Wright remembered the bushrangers, Martin Cash and Rheuben Priest, in their "respectable" days at Glenorchy.

Mr. Wright states that his remark had no reference to Mr. Rheuben Priest who died at Glenorchy about two years ago.

"The Mercury" joins with Mr. Wright in expressing regret for any offence that was unwittingly caused to Mr. Rheuben Priest's widow and family.

From: The Mercury, Hobart, Tuesday 24 Sep 1940 p5 and Saturday 28 Sep 1940 p5

28. See http://www.mitchamcouncil.sa.gov.au/webdata/resources/files/Anglican_Cemetery.pdf for a description of the cemetery which holds many South Australian pioneers. Below from http://ehlt.flinders.edu.au/archaeology/monuments/gravestones_detail.php?cemid=505

Cemetery Detail : Wright, Mitcham Anglican Cemetery

Grave Reference: 22
Surname: Wright
Site Location: Mitcham Anglican Cemetery
Cemetery: Mitcham General
Denomination: Unknown
Orientation : East
Associated plots :
Headstone Length (cm) : 7
Headstone Width (cm) : 81
Headstone Height (cm) : 180
Form : Tablet,
Footstone : No
Material : Granite,
Fence :
Fence Height (cm): 68
Other Items : None,
Lettering : Lead,
Motifs : None,
Language : Factual,
Tense : Third Person,
Described in Relation To: Family Position,
Keywording : In Memory of..,
Extra Information :
large site, writing on both sides of headstone

Date Recorded : 10/09/2010
Recorded By : Nathanael Koch
UserFAN : koch0053
CemId : 505

Inscription

In memory of Lucy Elizabeth,
wife of Stephen Amand Wright
of Lockleys near Adelaide
Died Sept 12th 1855
Aged 66 years

And of the above
Stephen Amand Wright
Died at Paris
March 2nd 1860
Aged 70 years.

29.

IGI Individual Record

FamilySearch™ International Genealogical Index v5.0
Southwest Pacific

Search Results | Download | Print

LUCY AMELIA WRIGHT
Female

Pedigree
Family

Event(s):
Birth:
Christening:
Death:
Burial:

Marriages:
Spouse: PETER DOWDING PRANKERD
Marriage: 08 MAR 1856 Christ Church, North Adelaide, South Australia, Australia

Family

Messages:
Extracted marriage record for locality listed in the record. The source records are usually arranged chronologically by the marriage date.

Source Information:

Batch No.:	Dates:	Source Call No.:	Type:	Printout Call No.:	Type:
M310081	1850 - 1880	0951889	Film	0883920	Film
Sheet: 00					

THE LATE MR. PRANKERD.

DIES IN ENGLAND.

London, December 22.

The death is announced at the age of 83 years of Mr. Peter Dowding Prankerd, who was well known in Adelaide business circles, but had for 30 years been residing at "The Knoll," Sneyd Park, near Bristol.

Mr. Prankerd was born in Taunton, Somerset, and at the age of 23 years came out to Sydney, whence, over half a century ago, he removed to Adelaide and entered into partnership with the late Mr. Robert Stuckey. He married in 1856 Miss Lucy Wright, of Lockleys. Mr. Prankerd was very successful in business, and at the time of his death was reputedly wealthy. He was a generous supporter of local institutions, and among other things he founded a scholarship at St. Peter's College. Mr. Prankerd possessed a large amount of property in this State.

Athelney House

RECENTLY members of the Pioneers' Association were entertained by Mr. and Mrs. Edgar Hughes at Athelney, Hackney, a handsome, two-storey stone house which Herbert Bristow Hughes purchased from P. D. Prankerd many years ago.

Yesterday the president (Mr. G. C. Morphett) told me something about Mr. Prankerd's career. Born at Langport, Somersetshire, in 1819, he went to sea and spent several years in the South Sea Islands, until he came to South Australia in 1850.

After a term in the land and estate agency business with Mr. Sam Lyons, he became a partner with Mr. Peter Stuckey in Gresham Chambers. Mr. Prankerd was prominently associated with the Wallaroo and Moonta copper mines. After several successful land speculations in Queensland, he amassed a considerable fortune, and in 1872 retired to England, where he purchased an estate called the Knoll, Sneyd Park, near Bristol. He endowed the Prankerd scholarship at St. Peter's College. On March 8, 1856, he married Miss Lucy Wright, of Lockleys, and resided at Athelney House. He was 83 when he died in England in December, 1902, leaving two sons and a daughter.

THE COMMEMORATION FESTIVAL.—It will be remembered that the unexpected rain which poured down on the 28th December, and which, by its interference with the festival prepared in commemoration of the foundation of the colony, gave new strength to the old proverb—

"The best-laid schemes o' mice and men
    Gang aft agley"—

had the effect of postponing the affixing of the engraved plate to the "Old Gum-tree" till some future time. That time arrived yesterday, 5 o'clock in the afternoon being the hour at which His Excellency the Governor-in-Chief had notified his desire to perform the ceremony. No public notice was given of this till yesterday morning, and the weather, so to speak, was taken quite aback. It had been so fine up to that moment that it could not with any propriety break off into a sudden storm on purpose, so it went on shining gloriously throughout the day. Punctually at the hour appointed His Excellency and Lady MacDonnell, attended by numerous ladies and gentlemen—amongst whom shone conspicuously four or five Commissariat officers, in their brilliant uniforms of blue and gold—arrived on the ground. There were then about 200 spectators present, many of whom were on horseback or in vehicles. As His Excellency arrived the Royal Standard which had been previously lowered, flung out its broad folds over the "Old Gum-Tree," and a brass band struck up a stirring strain of music. His Excellency ascended the platform, which was erected at the side of the tree, attended by the Hon. J. H. Fisher, the Hon. J. Morphett, Mr. S. Wright, the Mayor of Glenelg, and Mr. Hector. The latter gentleman presented the title-deeds of the land on which the tree stood to the Mayor of Glenelg. He said he had no doubt that the Corporation would faithfully preserve that tree of liberty, and the spot of ground on which it stood, as memorials of the founding of this colony. He hoped that many glorious commemorations of this event would be held on the same spot and when the tree had fallen to decay, and was crumbled in the dust, he trusted that South Australia would still run the career of progress upon which it had entered, and was now pursuing. The Mayor of Glenelg received the deeds, and remarked that he had no doubt but that the present and future Corporations of the town would thoroughly fulfil the trust reposed in them. Mr. Fisher received the plate with the inscription on the part of the colonists at large, for whom on this occasion he had, with great pride to himself, been taken as the mouthpiece, and he would, without comment, request His Excellency the Governor-in-Chief to affix the plate to the tree. He was sure that he expressed the feeling of the colonists at large when he said that the more firmly His Excellency attached the plate to the tree, the more firmly would he be regarded as being attached to South Australia. His Excellency would take the liberty to remark that, however agreeable it was to him that this pleasant duty should occur during his administration, he felt that there was one drawback in connection with it, and that was, the fact that the ceremony did not take place on the anniversary day. He could not but feel that he was guilty of an anachronism in affixing a plate on the 26th February which purported in its inscription to have been affixed on the 28th December. (Laughter.) He could assure them that, although he did not possess the privilege of hunting-ground, and forced into new relations, into new difficulties, into new quarrels, in consequence. Certainly he was a man who had no idea whatever that he was committing a crime which society has justly marked with its severest reprobation. On the contrary, he seems to think that he was only ridding society of a monster in plunging his avenging knife into the heart of "Wilddog." As British troops go forth to avenge upon sepoy ruffians the blood of their victims, so does Piulta represent himself as avenging upon the person of Wilddog the blood of the victims of that savage. Police-trooper Clarke deposes that when he went to apprehend Piulta, the latter expressed his astonishment, remarking that the policeman must be "a fool" for taking him, because he had killed Wilddog, and further remarking that Wilddog had killed his (Piulta's) brother, and that he had also killed many white men in order to steal their clothes. When on his trial Piulta justified his conduct on the ground that Wilddog had murdered several men belonging to the tribe of Piulta. Now, is it possible that we can hang a man for this? So far as the evidence goes, it only shows that Piulta, the savage, had killed a greater savage than himself, and one, moreover, who had murdered the brother of the avenger. According to the rude codes of early nations there is nothing criminal in such an act. Under the Mosaic dispensation was not the next of kin *required* to avenge the violent death of a relative; and can Christians hang the barbarian Piulta for doing what was an obligation of law under the more advanced civilisation of Moses? We know it will be said that the natives are now subject to British laws: that they enjoy the protection of those laws as well as suffer their infliction. But it is impossible to regard the aborigines in the full light of British subjects. They do not understand the applicability of our laws to their own wild habits. They may easily be made to understand that they must not plunder, assault, or kill *white* men; and as they can be made to understand the enormity of this, so they may be held amenable to the laws of the land in reference to such acts. But in the bush, away from civilisation, roaming naked in their unvisited solitudes, thinking little of English laws or English habits, the aborigines of Australia are hardly fitted to assume the responsibilities of British citizens in their disputes and quarrels with one another. They hold life cheaply; and although it is highly incumbent upon us to teach them its sacredness, we cannot hope to impress them with the same horror of bloodshed that we feel ourselves. Under these circumstances, to hang Piulta would be to inflict death upon a man who has not committed a crime which his race regard as atrocious; and whose act, though justly condemned by us, is not, in his eyes, a crime at all. We know not whether the Acting Chief Justice has recommended His Excellency to spare this man's life; and we have seen it somewhere intimated that without such a recommendation it would not be "etiquette" for the Governor to interfere. But surely a man's life is not to hang upon a point of "etiquette?" We cannot believe that Piulta will be executed. His Honor the Acting Chief Justice has often wished for the restoration of the Grand Jury. We yesterday published the presentment of the South Australian Grand Jury of 1851, in which will be found many sound and powerful arguments in favor of extending that clemency to native criminals which we now invoke for Piulta.—*Register*.—

31. http://adbonline.anu.edu.au/biogs/AS10500b.htm

32.

The South Australian Advertiser (Adelaide, SA : 1858-1889) — Friday 20 May 1859, Page 3 of 4

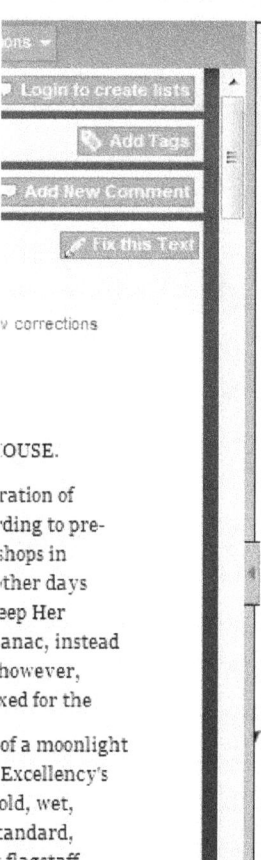

CELEBRATION OF HER MAJESTY'S BIRTHDAY.

LEVEE AND BALL AT GOVERNMENT HOUSE.

On Thursday, May 19, the official celebration of Her Majesty's birthday took place, according to previous proclamation in the *Gazette*. The shops in town were for the most part open as on other days—the citizens of Adelaide preferring to keep Her Majesty's birthday according to the almanac, instead of according to the *Gazette*. We believe, however, that the Government celebration was fixed for the 19th, in order to secure the advantages of a moonlight night for the homeward journeys of His Excellency's guests upon the occasion. The day was cold, wet, and dreary; but the sight of the Royal Standard, floating from the top of the Government flagstaff, attracted a considerable number of persons in the vicinity of its glories, and as the hour of noon approached, a fair stream of Her Majesty's liege subjects might have been observed wending their way toward the scene of action. A little prior to the holding of the levee, a military demonstration on a small scale took place in the paddock fronting the Police Barracks, and before the noon-day gun was fired, the visitors at the levee were in pretty good force on the ground. The order of proceedings varied in nothing particular from former occasions. His Excellency and suite were assembled in one of the rooms in the eastern wing of Government House, visitors entering at the eastern door, and after exchanging salutations with His Excellency, passing out at the principal entrance.

The following are the names of the gentlemen who attended

THE MORNING LEVEE.

Mr. R. F. Minchin, Mr. Henry Morri[s], Mr. James Macgeorge, Mr. Malcolm, Mr. R. F. Newland, Major Nelson, Mr. and Mrs. Nation, Dr. and Mrs. Nugent.

Mrs. and Miss O'Halloran, Mr. T. O'Halloran, Mr. G. O'Halloran, Mr. H. O'Halloran, Captain and Mrs. O'Halloran, Mr. J. S. O'Halloran, Mr. and Mrs. Oldham, Mr. and Mrs. Ormerod, Mr. John Ormerod.

Mr. and Mrs. James Phillips, Mr. and Mrs. Peterswald, Mr. E. J. Peake, M.P., Mr. and Mrs. Parr, Mr. and Mrs. Joseph Peacock, Mr. Pitts, Mr. and Mrs. G. Perry, Mr. and Mrs. Peter, Mrs. H. Price, Mr. and Mrs. D. Power, Mt. Poole.

Mr. and Mrs. Quick.

Mr. and Mrs. O. K. Richardson and Miss Richardson, Mr. W. Randell, Mr. Reynolds, M.P., and Mrs. Reynolds, Rev. Mr. and Mrs. Ross, Mr. and Mrs. D. Randell.

Mr. and Mrs. Singleton, the Hon. A. Scott, M.L.C., Mr. G. Stevenson, Mr. and Mrs. Frederick Sanderson, Mr. and Mrs. R. J. Stow, Mr. H. E. Smith, Mr. and Mrs. Sholl, Mr. and Mrs. Henry Seymour and Miss Seymour, Mr. G. B. Scott, Mr. and Mrs. R. B. Smith, Mr. Strangways, M.P., Mr. Square, Mr. T. Seymour, Mr. Spence, the Hon. Edward Stirling, M.L.C., and Mrs. Stirling, Mr. and Mrs. G. B. Smith, Mr. R. Seymour, Mr. and Mrs. Sinnett, Mr. Surtees.

Mr. and Mrs. John Taylor, Miss Taylor, Mr. and Mrs. R. R. Torrens, Mr. and Mrs. Charles Thompson, Mr. and Mrs. S. Tomkinson, Mr. and Mrs. Trimmer, Mr. and Mrs. Henry E. Thompson, Mr. and Madame Turner, Mr. and Mrs. G. Tinline, Mr. and Mrs. C. Todd, Mr. and Mrs. Thrupp.

Mr. and Mrs. Woodforde, Captain and Mrs. Watts, Dr. and Mrs. Wyatt, Mr. W. Wyatt, Mr. and Mrs. Wooldridge, Major and Mrs. Warburton, Mr. Percival Warburton, Mrs. and the Misses Wigley, Mr. W. R. Wigley, Mr. T. Wigley, Mr. Wildman, Mr. Wearing, Mr. and Mrs. Alfred Watts, Mr. Worthington, Mr. G. Worthington, jun., Mr. and Mrs. John Williams, Mr. and Mrs. Stephen Wright, Mr. Frederick Wright, Mr. and Mrs. Edmund W. Wright, Mr. and Mrs. Arthur Wright, Mr. and Mrs. E. A. Wright, Mr. and Mrs. Samuel Wright, Mr. Edwin White, Miss Elizabeth White, Mr. and Mrs. G. M. Waterhouse, Mr. Thomas Wells, Mrs. White, Mr. and the Misses Wilson, Mr. Andrew Watson, Mr. Thomas Walters, Miss Waylen.

The Hon. W. Younghusband, M.L.C., Mrs. and Miss Younghusband, Mr. John Young, Miss Young, Mr. and Mrs. George Young, Mr. and Mrs. Barney Young, Mr. Gavin Young. Mr. George Young.

THE REAL PROPERTY ACT.

DINNER TO MR. TORRENS AT CLARE.

On Tuesday, the 17th May, Mr. Torrens met with a reception from the settlers of the district of Clare, of which he may well be proud. The weather during the day was boisterous, and it rained frequently from an early hour. At 2 o'clock

33. See note 28 above and

The South Australian Advertiser (Adelaide, SA : 1858-1889) — Monday 7 May 1860, Page 2 of 4

BIRTH.

February 29, at Cressington Park, near Liverpool, Mrs. Samuel R. Kearne, of a son.

DIED.

March 2, at Paris, in the 71st year of his age, Stephen Amand Wright, Esq., late of Lockleys, near Adelaide.

34.

The South Australian Advertiser (Adelaide, SA : 1858-1889) — Saturday 18 November 1865, Page 1 of 4

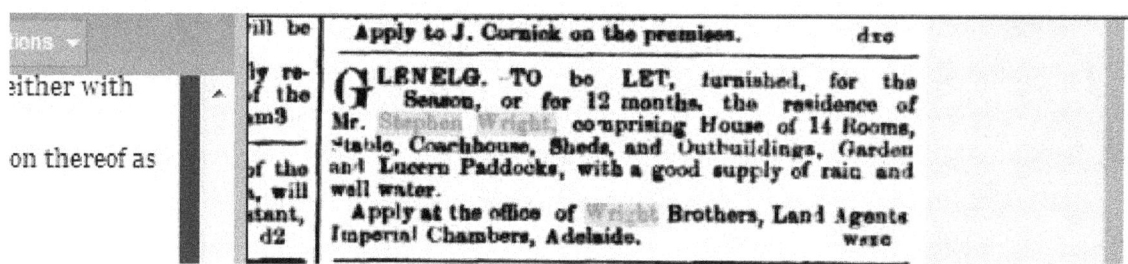

Apply to J. Cornick on the premises.

GLENELG.—TO be LET, furnished, for the Season, or for 12 months, the residence of Mr. Stephen Wright, comprising House of 14 Rooms, Stable, Coachhouse, Sheds, and Outbuildings, Garden and Lucern Paddocks, with a good supply of rain and well water.

Apply at the office of Wright Brothers, Land Agents Imperial Chambers, Adelaide.

35. See http://books.google.com/books?id=v279uRHojcMC&pg=PA17&lpg=PA17&dq=steamer+%22Derwent%22+Melbourne&source=bl&ots=dk3xv7zEFp&sig=8uEfliTn-OCnOtX1lXzaqQehoCc&hl=en&ei=kJ3tTNrON86fOp-7xFc&sa=X&oi=book_result&ct=result&resnum=1&ved=0CBMQ6AEwAA#v=onepage&q=steamer%20%22Derwent%22%20Melbourne&f=false

and http://www.flotilla-australia.com/melbsc.htm#derwent-msc ,

plus http://www.flotilla-australia.com/bluemu.htm#coorong-bluemu .

36.

The Mercury, Wednesday Mar 4, 1868 page 1.

MARINE RESIDENCE.

TO VISITORS FROM THE NEIGHBORING COLONIES IN SEARCH OF HEALTH.

An opportunity now occurs for the purchase of a most delightful residence, with the advantage of sea bathing.

THE GROVE ESTATE,

Containing nearly 46 acres of the richest land in Tasmania, situate at O'Brien's Bridge, 5 miles from Hobart Town, and on the main line of road from Hobart Town to Launceston. The whole of the land can be irrigated at pleasure by a never-failing stream of water. For hop-growing it would be invaluable. The garden contains about 2 acres, and is stocked with the choicest fruit trees.

The mansion is suited for a family of the first respectability.

For further particulars as to terms, &c., apply to the undersigned,

ROBT. BENNISON,
Exchange Chambers.

2nd March, 1868.   mws tc

Chapter 2

1. Much of the early history of Glenorchy written here has been taken with kind permission from Glenorchy City Council directly from Alison Alexander's book "Glenorchy 1804-1964". The maps generated by Mollie Tomlin provide visual references for the setting of this story.

HOBART TOWN GAZETTE, and SOUTHERN REPORTER:
PUBLISHED BY AUTHORITY.
Vol. IV.]   SATURDAY, JULY 10, 1819.   [No. 164.

FOR SALE by PRIVATE CONTRACT, that beautiful Farm known by the Name of Montrose, consisting of 120 Acres, situate about 4 Miles from Hobart Town; is convenient for land or water carriage, is bounded on the North by the River Derwent, on the East by Humphrey's Rivulet (a detachment of which runs within 30 yards of the house which is erected upon the Estate), and affords an ample supply of water for domestic purposes at all seasons of the year.—Likewise, a Quantity of Horned Cattle on reasonable Terms.—For further Particulars apply to ROBERT OGILVIE on the Premises.

2.

Hobart Town Gazette and Van Diemen's Land Advertiser (Tas. : 1821-1825) about ◀ Saturday 1 September 1821 ▶ ◀ Page 2 S ▼ of 4

3.—That most desirable Freehold Estate, called Montrose Farm, formerly the Property of the late Mr. Littlejohn, containing upwards of 100 Acres, of which several Acres are in Cultivation. situate in the same District, only 5 Miles from Town, contiguous to Humphrey's River, and adjoining the New Road also. This Farm, which is one of the most picturesque and delightful Situations in the Neighbourhood, is in every Respect truly valuable, but more particularly on Account of the vast Quantity of fine Timber, fit for every Kind of Building, which is growing upon it.—It also possesses a singularly pleasant Prospect of the River Derwent; is remarkably well situated for Land and Water Carriage, and always abundantly supplied with excellent Water. There is a neat little Cottage, weather-boarded, shingled, and glazed, erected upon it, and a Garden well stocked with choice Fruit Trees

3. The Hobart Town Courier (Tas.: 1827-1839) — Saturday 10 March 1832, Page 3 of 4

ELIGIBLE OPPORTUNITY FOR INVESTING CAPITAL IN VALUABLE ESTATES AND FARMS.

TO BE SOLD BY PUBLIC AUCTION.

BY MR. W. COOK,

On Tuesday the 20th March inst, at his Mart in Elizabeth-st.,

By order of the Sheriff,

Positively without reserve, the following most eligible PROPERTIES, viz:—

ALL that beautiful and valuable Estate called MONTROSE, situate at O'Brien's bridge, 5 miles from Hobart town, fronting the river Derwent, and bounded on one side by that excellent fresh water stream called 'Humphrey's rivulet,' which empties itself into the Derwent at this farm, and is capable of carrying upon it several mills. The high road runs northward through the estate from O'Brien's bridge, giving a frontage on both sides of the road. This estate contains 120 acres by grant, and a marsh given in, making 148 acres, of which 30 acres are in cultivation; the whole fenced in, and having upon it a capital two-story brick dwelling-house, lately finished in a superior style, cottage, out-houses, &c. This estate is adapted for a genteel residence with extensive pleasure grounds, commanding rich land and water scenery, and for dividing into allotments, being in the immediate vicinity where land is now selling in small portions at L30 per acre. The timber on part of the estate is highly valuable, and vessels of 30 to 40 tons burthen can unload within a hundred yards of the house.

ALSO.—

4. The Hobart Town Courier (Tas.: 1827-1839) — Saturday 24 March 1832, Page 2 of 4

At the Sheriff's sale of Mr. Stocker's property on Tuesday, the beautiful estate of Montrose at O'Brien's bridge was bought by Mr. Robertson, lately from India, at L1100; the farm of 100 acres at Cray-fish point was sold for L110; that at Stony point ferry, 60 acres for L420; the farm of 200 acres at Ross Bridge at L600, the allotment in the

5. The Hobart Town Courier (Tas.: 1827-1839) — Saturday 28 January 1832, Page 1 of 4

FAMILY RESIDENCE.

TO BE LET, and possession given on the 17th instant, that elegant and commodious Cottage residence, situate in Macquarie-st, formerly in the occupation of Captain Briggs, and fit for the immediate reception of a genteel family. There is an abundant supply of water, and every other convenience on the premises. For Further particulars apply on the premises, or to Mr. Butler, Solicitor, Hobart-town.

Jan. 6, 1832.

6.

The Hobart Town Courier (Tas.: 1827-1839)   Friday 23 May 1834   Page 3 of 4

Hobart-town, May 17, 1834.

Sir,—

We, the undersigned, request you will be pleased to convene a public meeting of the free inhabitants of the colony, to take into consideration the necessity of addressing His Excellency the Lieutenant Governor, that he will be pleased to refuse his sanction to the introduction of any measure with the Legislative Council, which may have for its object, any limitation of numbers or restriction of qualifications of a Jury, beyond that established by British law, it being avowed by the Attorney General, that he proposes to reduce the old established British number of 12 jurymen to 7 in this colony.

We are, Sir, your obedient servants,

James Hackett	James Kelly
J. Swan	John Dunn
Henry Melville	R. L. Murray
Henry Hilton	Robert Kerr
Samuel Bryan	F. W. Rowlands
John Bryan	Wallace Murdoch
A. Dennis Bryan	John Briggs
Wm. Gellibrand	Thomas Richards
Thomas M. Fenton	Gilbert Robertson
John Bell	Thomas A. Lascelles
R. W. Loane	Charles B. Lyons
Anthony F. Kemp	W. Wilson
George Cartwright	Thomas Horne
Thomas Hewitt	William Bryan
James Smith.	

To Thomas Bannister, esq. Sheriff of Van Diemen's land, &c.

In pursuance of the above requisition, I hereby convene a meeting of the inhabitants of this colony, at the Court house, Hobart town, on Monday the 9th day of June next, at 12 o'clock precisely, for the purpose of taking the matters in the requisition named into consideration.

THOMAS BANNISTER, Sheriff.

Sheriff's office, May 22, 1834.

7.

Colonial Times (Hobart, Tas.: 1828-1857)   Tuesday 29 May 1838   Page 1 of 8

To be Sold by Private Contract.

A SMALL FARM, of about 130 Acres, with DWELLING-HOUSE &c. adjoining Mr. Barclay's, late Captain Briggs', only **FIVE MILES FROM TOWN**,

This may be a very good opportunity for any industrious person. The greatest part of the purchase money may remain on mortgage. For further particulars, enquire of

WILSON & TONKIN,

Liverpool-street, May 25, 1838.   (5419)

8. Alison Alexander "Glenorchy 1804 – 1964" p 15

9. The Courier (Hobart, Tas. : 1840-1859)   Friday 8 March 1844   Page 3 of 4

Horses, Milch Cows, Stacks of Hay, Farming Implements, &c.

MR. T. Y. LOWES will SELL by AUCTION, at the Grove Estate, O'Brien's Bridge, On WEDNESDAY, the 13th instant, at 12 o'clock precisely, by order of the administratrix to the estate of the late William Morgan Orr, Esq.—

- Two powerful cart horses
- One carriage horse
- One saddle do
- One pony mare
- Five very superior milch cows
- Six very excellent carriage and cart horses, just broken in
- One stack new hay, about 70 tons
- Two stacks old do, about 30 tons
- One four-wheel carriage
- One gig and harness
- Three carts, two ploughs, one winnowing machine, one roller
- One pair harrows, one cucumber frame
- Two breeding sows
- Ten sheep
- Forty turkeys, geese, &c.
- Two hundred fowls
- With a quantity of agricultural implements, tools, &c.

AND

One boat, sails, and oars

Terms—Three months' credit above £25.

☞ The purchaser of the hay will be allowed six weeks to remove it.

10. Alison Alexander "Glenorchy 1804 – 1964" p 30

11. Colonial Times (Hobart, Tas. : 1828-1857)   Tuesday 24 September 1844   Page 2 of 4

DIED—On the 19th instant, at his residence, O'Brien's Bridge, Captain John George Briggs.

DIED—On the 2nd day of May last, at her residence, Bury-street, London, after an illness of two years, Elizabeth Moses, mother of Mr. David Moses, Liverpool-street, Hobart Town, aged 78 years, leaving a husband and a numerous family, the greater number of whom are in these colonies, to regret her loss.

12. Colonial Times (Hobart, Tas. : 1828-1857)   Tuesday 21 December 1847   Page 2 of 4

FOR SALE,

THE GROVE ESTATE, O'Brien's Bridge, containing 45 acres of rich alluvial soil, with entrance lodge; eight acres of English grass under irrigation; the remainder can be irrigated at a trifling expense. The Garden is well stocked with the choicest fruit trees. The House is in excellent repair, and consists of ten well-proportioned rooms, detached kitchens, dairy, and extensive out-buildings.—For further particulars, and cards to view, apply to Mr. J. L. Stewart, Davey-street Brewery.

December 14, 1847.   2681

13. Colonial Times (Hobart, Tas. : 1828-1857) — Friday 6 April 1849, Page 3 of 4

Notice.

IF all accounts, which remain unsettled in respect to J. P. Lester, are not immediately paid, will be handed over to the Solicitors for recovery.

The Grove, Kensington,
April 5, 1849. 827

14. Colonial Times (Hobart, Tas. : 1828-1857) — Tuesday 19 May 1857, Page 2 of 4

MARRIED.

On the 14th inst., by the Rev. Wm. Nicolson, at the residence of the bride's father, JOHN FRANKLIN OCTAVIUS, eighth son of George Hull, Esq., of Tolosa, to MARY ANN, the amiable, accomplished and only daughter of J. P. Lester, Esq., of the Grove, Kensington, O'Brien's Bridge.

15. The Mercury (Hobart, Tas. : 1860-1954) — Monday 23 December 1867, Page 1 of 4

DEATHS.

LESTER.—On the 21st of December, at the Grove, Glenorchy, John Providence Lester, Esq., aged 68 years. The funeral will leave his late residence on Tuesday, 24th instant, at 4 o'clock, p.m. Friends will please accept this invitation, as no circulars will be issued. 24d

16.

MARINE RESIDENCE.

TO VISITORS FROM THE NEIGHBORING COLONIES IN SEARCH OF HEALTH.

An opportunity now occurs for the purchase of a most delightful residence, with the advantage of sea bathing.

THE GROVE ESTATE,

Containing nearly 46 acres of the richest land in Tasmania, situate at O'Brien's Bridge, 5 miles from Hobart Town, and on the main line of road from Hobart Town to Launceston. The whole of the land can be irrigated at pleasure by a never-failing stream of water. For hop-growing it would be invaluable. The garden contains about 2 acres, and is stocked with the choicest fruit trees.

The mansion is suited for a family of the first respectability.

For further particulars as to terms, &c., apply to the undersigned,

ROBT. BENNISON,
Exchange Chambers.

2nd March, 1868. mws tc

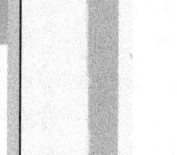

Y MORNING, DECEMBER 11, 1868.

Town Hall that over 1,200 persons had voted.

GLENORCHY.

The election of Councillors for the above municipality resulted in the return of the following gentlemen:—

	Votes.
Bilton	94
Brent	93
Wright	57
Buck	52

RICHMOND.

Hobart Town at the above Cathedral at

7 O'CLOCK A.M.

be preached after the first Gospel, and a

MADE at the OFFERTORY.

JOSEPH'S CHOIR

their assistance for the occasion.

[ADVERTISEMENT.]

L ELECTION.

EDITOR OF THE MERCURY.

...andidates for municipal honors ...nated in the Sorell District, ...ar to have arisen from some Mr. Allison saying that he ... one to vote for him, on Dr. ...t he would not solicit any votes, ...n announcing that he wished ...be voted for, and in the re-Coram.

...ry that the office held by Mr. ...contested for apart from the ...iring Councillors—Dunbabin, ...th—who were eligible for re-...vertisements were plain on this ...one who read them; hence ...Jenkins was duly returned as ...not being opposed in seeking ...ld by Mr. Coram, the election ...extraordinary one.

...new candidates give out that ...ld to oppose the return of Mr. ...Blyth; they plainly say they ... vacant seat. This being the ...d the electors do? I, as an ...s advice, be it taken or not, ...es; they are known, and have ...r good and bad qualities are ...ctors; I, as well as others, do ...hem in all things. But what ...n who wish to become public ... more *intelligent!* Are they ...re satisfaction and less trouble ... have done.

AN ELECTOR.

Bull, Thomas Allwright, and James Wilshire, of New Norfolk.

Dated at the Municipal Chamber, New Norfolk, this 3rd day of December, 1868.

W. A. B. JAMIESON,

4,8d   Warden, Returning Officer.

RURAL MUNICIPALITY OF GLENORCHY.

NOTICE IS HEREBY GIVEN, that the following Municipal Electors have this day been nominated to me for Election as Councillors of the above Municipality:—

BILTON, HENRY, of Claremont, Glenorchy, Freeholder, nominated by H. S. Barrett, Esq., J. A. Dunn, Esq., C. M. Maxwell, Esq., and seven other Electors.

BRENT, JOHN, of Roseneath, Glenorchy, Freeholder, nominated by Thos. Y. Lowes, Esq., J. A. Dunn, Esq., C. M. Maxwell, Esq., and twelve other Electors.

BUCK, FREDERICK, of Davey-street, Hobart, Freeholder, nominated by T. Y. Lowes, Esq., J. A. Dunn, Esq., C. M. Maxwell, Esq., and twelve other Electors.

WRIGHT, STEPHEN PELTRO HENRY, of the Grove, Glenorchy, Freeholder, nominated by T. Y. Lowes, Esq., T. G. Reed, Esq., George Hall, Esq., and three other Municipal Electors.

HENRY BUTLER,
Warden.

Glenorchy,
3rd December, 1868.   8s 6d

GREEN, WILLIAM

HINSBY, HENRY,

LEWIS, DAVID,

18.

 http://gw0.geneanet.org/index.php3?b=alivornesi&lang=en&m=AM&v=8

Leghorn Merchant Networks

Check also the Leghorn Merchant Networks Project Blog.
This research is self-financed, all work has been done by myself since year 2000.
If you have information, questions or corrections please contact me by the e-mail you find in the Contact Pag to cite me.
A big 'thank you' to all people who cooperated and corrected the data.

Anniversaries of marriage in August

- Henry Dunkin O'HALLORAN and Mona Jane WRIGHT, in 1874

19. See http://search.archives.tas.gov.au/default.aspx?detail=1&type=A&id=NG01420
20.

Gravesites Of Tasmania

Home | Rev Dr Drought | Church History | Maps & Burials

St Pauls Anglican Glenorchy

Surname	Christian Names	Date of Death	Date of Burial	Age	Occupation	Residence
Wright	Katherine Maria	08 Dec 1895	10 Dec 1895	45	Wife of Orchardist	Glenorchy
Wright	Elizabeth Jane	16 Apr 1884	18 Apr 1884		Wife of S.P.H. Wright	Glenorchy
Wright	Stephen Peltro Henry	15 Sep 1886	17 Sep 1886	67	Gentleman	Glenorchy

http://gravesoftas.dyndns.org/Graves%20of%20Tasmania/Church%20maps%20&%20Burials/Registers/St.%20Paul's%20Burial%20Register.htm

21.

IGI Individual Record

FamilySearch™ International Genealogical Index v5.0

Search Results | Download | Print

Southwest Pacific

Harold Stephen Robert Wright
Male

Pedigree
Family

Event(s):
Birth:
Christening:
Death:
Burial:

Parents:
Father: Stephen Peltro Henry Wright
Mother: Elizabeth Jane Howard

Family

Marriages:
Spouse: Katharine Maria Chapman
Marriage: 01 OCT 1884 Hobart, Tasmania, Australia

Family

Messages:
Record submitted after 1991 by a member of the LDS Church. No additional information is available. Ancestral File may list the same family and the submitter.

Source Information:
No source information is available.

22. See note 20 above and

    The Mercury (Hobart, Tas. : 1860-1954) — Saturday 18 September 1886 — Page 1 S of 6

    > WEBB.—On September 8, 1886, at Hobart, after a short but painful illness, Thomas William, son of Louisa and the late Wm. Webb, of Bagdad, aged 27 years.
    > WRIGHT.—On Wednesday, September 15, at his late residence, the Grove, Glenorchy, Stephen Peltro Henry Wright.

23.

TASMANIA
The Births, Deaths and Marriages Registration Act 1999

Registration No. 759/1888

RECORD OF MARRIAGE

MARRIAGES solemnized in the District of HOBART

Number	194 / 447	
When and Where Married	24 October 1888 CATHEDRAL CHURCH OF ST. DAVID, HOBART	
Name and Surname	Howard Edward WRIGHT	Maude Florence ROGERS
Age	38 Years	27 Years
Rank	Gentleman	Daughter of Barrister
Description of Parties	Bachelor	Spinster
Name of Clergyman, Officiating Minister or Registrar	Alfred N. Masor	
When Registered	24 October 1888	

Married according to the Rites and Ceremonies of THE CHURCH OF ENGLAND by LICENCE with consent of Not Stated.

(In the presence of us) John ROBERTS
                         G.S. CHAPMAN

Additional Information
Additional Witness: Harold F.P. Wright.

I CERTIFY THIS TO BE A COPY OF AN ENTRY IN A REGISTER OR RECORD KEPT BY ME, GIVEN IN PURSUANCE OF THE ACTS OF PARLIAMENT OF THE STATE OF TASMANIA THIS 16 DECEMBER, 2009.

E. Ann Owen

Ann Owen DELEGATE FOR REGISTRAR OF BIRTHS DEATHS AND MARRIAGES

Maude was born in 1861 in Sydney to Edward and Eliza (Taylor) Rogers. Both parents had migrated from England as Free Settlers in the 1830s. Edward was a successful Solicitor and Eliza was an accomplished, but unpublicized, artist. Their lives are detailed in "Free Settlers and Convicts in Early Australia. A Short History of the Dents and the Taylors 1663 – 2010", by Warren Dent, Infinity Publishing, 2010

24. The Mercury (Hobart, Tas. : 1860-1954) Thursday 13 June 1889 Page 1 of 4

Marriages.

WRIGHT—BUTLER.—On June 8, at All Saints' Church, Ernest Charles Wright, of "The Grove," Glenorchy, to Kate A., eldest daughter of the late Hon. Henry Butler, of Hobart.

25. The Mercury (Hobart, Tas. : 1860-1954) Friday 24 January 1890 Page 4

GLENORCHY POLICE COURT.

The Warden (Mr. H. S. R. Wright) and Councillor Murray presided at the Glenorchy Police Court yesterday.

BREACH OF LICENSING ACT.—Michael Tuttle, John Tuttle, the younger, George Philips, Thomas Johnston, the younger, and Kenoth McKay were charged with on Sunday last being in the Racecourse Hotel, occupied by Catherine McDonald. The first three defendants pleaded guilty, and the last two not guilty. The cases against McKay and Johnston were then dealt with. Constable William Clements said he was on duty at Glenorchy on Sunday last, and saw McKay and Johnston going into the back yard of the hotel. He believed they went into the house, and he then reported the matter to Sub-Inspector Wallace who went with him into the house by the back way. Did not see the defendants in the house when he and Wallace went in. Wallace and he then left the Hotel, and found the defendants on the road. When witness served the summons on Johnston he admitted being in the house. About five minutes elapsed between the defendants entering the yard and witness following them. In answer to Johnston the constable said he would not be positive whether Johnston told him he was on the premises or in the house. George Philips, one of the defendants, who pleaded guilty, said neither McKay nor Johnston were in the hotel while he was in on Sunday. Johnston and McKay were dismissed, and penalties of 5s. each and costs, in default seven days, were inflicted on the other defendants.

26. Current holdover of a Worker's hut in Main St, Glenorchy

27. http://books.google.com/books?id=3oDNAAAAMAAJ&pg=PA346&lpg=PA346&dq=Tasmanian+Exhibition+1894-5&source=bl&ots=tz8UWRynLs&sig=ARYVjVKGM8rd-HwLdlt70LZ2H-g&hl=en&ei=liL7S7bQA8aqlAelqcW3DW&sa=X&oi=book_result&ct=result&resnum=8&ved=0CC0Q6AEwBw#v=onepage&q=Tasmanian%20Exhibition%201894-5&f=false

TASMANIAN INTERNATIONAL EXHIBITION OF 1894-5.

The following is the text of the prospectus of an International Exhibition which is to be held in Hobart during the summer of 1894-95:—

It has been decided to hold an International Exhibition in Hobart during the summer of 1894-95 and the Government of Tasmania has granted their official patronage to the undertaking.

The proposal has been taken up by the people of Tasmania and the adjacent colonies with such general approval that the necessary capital has been most readily subscribed.

The city of Hobart is most favourably situated. The colony of Tasmania has a population of 150,000, and with the neighbouring colonies the total population numbers about 4,000,000 inhabitants. Launceston and other centres are within a few hours by rail. The Australian colonies are easy of access by steam, and the tourist's routes to all places of interest radiate from Hobart.

The objects of the Exhibition are:—To promote and foster industry, science, and art, by inciting the inventive genius of the people to a further improvement in arts and manufactures, as well as to stimulate commercial enterprise by inviting all nations to exhibit their products both in the raw and finished state. Samples of the products for which this and the other Australasian colonies have become famous will be exhibited with a view to increase the development of their natural resources.

Similar and more varied exhibits may be expected from Great Britain, the Continent of Europe, America, India, Canada, the Cape, and other colonies, to which the Government of Tasmania have forwarded an official invitation to grant their substantial support to the undertaking.

A fine-art section will form an important and attractive department of the exhibition. For the accommodation of the art treasures and historical objects a special block of the building will be reserved, and the most ample precautions will be taken for the security of valuable property lent for the purposes of the exhibition.

Two sections, viz., the Women's Industrial and the Artisan Section will be particular features. Special arrangements will be made for the management of these.

The site which has been granted by the Government for the exhibition buildings covers about 11 acres. It is one of exceptional beauty and convenience, being that portion of the Queen's domain adjoining the battery and the Central Railway Station.

The buildings which it is proposed to erect will be constructed according to plans prepared by competent architects. The ornamental flower pots, shrubberies, fountains, &c. will be enclosed in the Exhibition grounds, where musical promenades and other entertainments will be provided for the enjoyment of visitors.

The situation of the Exhibition buildings is specially convenient of access for exhibitors by means of the lines of rail which can be made use of day or night for the passage of railway trucks. Heavy goods can be delivered at a minimum cost, and with the least possible amount of risk. In addition to this, the port of Hobart offers a cheap and ready means for the receiving and delivery of all sea-borne goods.

It is intended to afford full postal, telephonic, telegraphic, and banking facilities within the Exhibition buildings, so that all necessary business may be conducted by exhibitors and others without leaving the premises.

The whole arrangements are in the hands of a powerful directorate, and everything will be done to facilitate the work of exhibitors, and minimise their outlay.

A full statement of the regulations for exhibitors and a detailed classification of exhibits may be seen on application at the Commercial Department, Board of Trade, S.W.

28. A letter from Kate Wright to a Mrs. Cameron living nearby at the property named Lowestoff written between 1890 and 1895 shows the Wrights helping raise funds to support local churches. The note says: Dear Mrs Cameron. A meeting takes place in the Sunday School on Friday next at half past three o'clock for the purpose of arranging some way of getting money to pay some of the Church debts. If possible I hope you will attend. Hoping to see you. Sincerely Yours Kate Wright

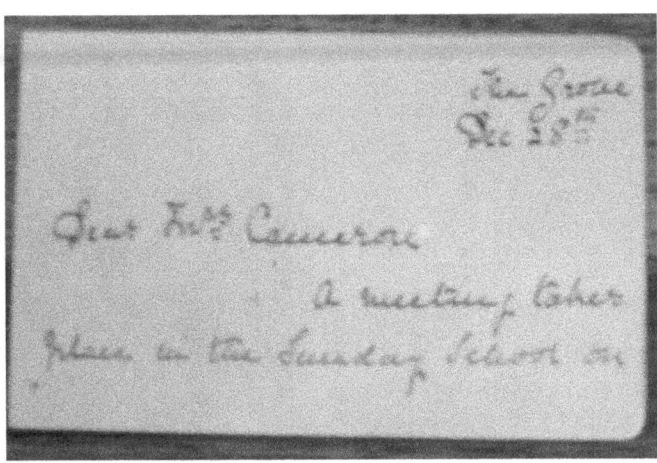

Friday next at half past three o'clock for the purpose of arranging some way of getting money to pay some of the Church debts if possible I hope you will attend Hoping to see you

Sincerely Yours

Kate Wright

29.

The Mercury (Hobart, Tas. : 1860-1954)   Tuesday 10 December 1895   Page 1 of 4

Deaths.

BROWN.—On October 6, 1895, at his residence, Milford, Salisbury, Wiltshire, England, Thomas Brown, Esq., aged 68 years. The above gentleman was for many years a settler at Longley, Huon-road, and subsequently resided in Upper Davey-street, Hobart.

BELBIN.—On December 7, at 16, Sackville-street, Norah, widow of the late William James Belbin, in the 52nd year of her age, respected by all who knew her. The Funeral will take place at 3 o'clock on TUESDAY AFTERNOON, when friends are respectfully invited. R.I.P.

NELSON.—At "Brighton Lodge," Harry Leslie Nelson, aged 24 years, fourth son of the late William Nelson, of Oatlands. Funeral will leave St. Peter's Church, Oatlands, at 3 p.m. on THIS DAY, 10th inst.

WRIGHT.—On Sunday, December 8, at her residence "The Grove," Glenorchy, Katherine Maria, wife of Harold Wright, and eldest daughter of the late T. D. Chapman, "Sunnyside."

EXCITEMENT AT HIGH NOON ON SATURDAY, AND, WITH SOME RELUCTANCE, WE CLOSED OUR DOORS WHEN THE ONE O'CLOCK GUN SOUNDED; FOR IT SEEMED AS THOUGH THE

30.

BEE CULTURE AT GLENORCHY.

In the Mother Country, and in nearly all the Australasian colonies, bee culture has been followed on an extensive scale, and the industrious insect made to yield its quota to the produce of the country. In Tasmania bees are kept by many people, but for the most part the owners do not extend operations beyond a few hives, and as a consequence the larger proportion of the honey consumed in this colony has to be imported. We are pleased to notice that Messrs. H. E. and E. C. Wright, The Grove, Glenorchy, have started operations with the view of enabling the colony to assume its proper place in regard to this industry. An apiary has been added to their extensive hop and orchard grounds, and everything arranged for the production of honey on a large scale. In this new departure Messrs. Wright have taken advantage of the experience gained in other colonies, notably New Zealand, where bee culture has arrived at a high state of perfection, and, discarding the old-fashioned modes of housing and caring for the bees, they have decided on adopting the latest improvements. Langstroth's patent hives, which are reckoned the most modern and approved, have been selected, and seem admirably adapted for the handling of the insect on a large scale, being commodious and so constructed that the combs of the industrious insect can be easily got at. Each hive is supplied with frames (10) which have artificial comb, stretching only about half-length over the frame. The utility of this is easily seen. The bees finding the comb ready to hand extend it without difficulty to the full length of the frame, and thus they are enabled to devote nearly all their time to the collection of honey. According to the old system much preliminary time would have been lost in making the comb. The next important consideration is the kind of bee to be kept, and the Messrs. Wright, after much consideration of the matter, have decided in favour of the Ligurian or Italian bee. At present they have 40 hives of this kind, and 35 of the common black bee, but it is their intention to gradually supplant the latter, and to go in for a pure stock of Ligurians. As compared with the black bee, the Ligurian is a prettier and livelier insect, with its beautiful golden stripes, and in addition to its attractions, it is to be preferred for its docility and extra working powers. It not only rises earlier than the black bee, but does not stick so closely to the native rule of knocking off at sundown, and the result is a much larger store of honey. At present the apiary, which, by-the-way, has been christened the "Marrinook Apiary," may be said to be yet in its infancy. It was only last season that the Messrs. Wright commenced that the Messrs. Wright commenced operations by raising swarms of Ligurians from a stock imported from Queensland, New Zealand, and New South Wales. Considering the short time that the apiary has been at work the yield this year has been very satisfactory, but it will be another season before the industry is in full swing, and by that time it is estimated there will be no fewer than 200 hives of pure Ligurians at work. A visit to the apiary is most interesting, and with such an enthusiast in bee culture as Mr. Ernest Wright, for cicerone, much is learned of the habits and work of the insect. The honey having been gathered the comb is transferred to a four-fold extractor—a new and improved machine—which works with great velocity, and empties the combs very expeditiously. A feature of the business is the scrupulous care taken to produce the honey pure. The wax is carefully paired off the comb before being placed in the extractor, and the honey, as it flows out, is perfectly clean and pure. Indeed, the quality of the honey in these respects cannot be surpassed, and it has received many encomiums from connoisseurs, and when the honey becomes known its good qualities should undoubtedly find for it a ready market. In addition to placing in the market ample supplies of honey, Messrs. Wright will be able next year to supply persons desirous of investing with pure stocks of Ligurian bees. This will be a great advantage. At present such stock has to be imported, which means an outlay in freight, and sometimes the entire loss of the stock in transit. Messrs. Wright recently imported two Queen bees from Sydney, which arrived dead, but had to be paid for all the same. A machine for manufacturing artificial comb will be shortly introduced, so that bee-keepers can be supplied with the useful and economical article, which contributes so much to the saving of labour and the wealth of the hive.

31. See "Glenorchy 1804-1964", by Alison Alexander, page 109

32.

The Mercury (Hobart, Tas. : 1860-1954) — Wednesday 17 December 1902 — Page 1 of 8

MARRIAGES.

WRIGHT—WAYN.—On December 5, at St. John's, Toorak, Victoria, Harold Stephen Robert Wright, of Glenorchy, to Mary Louisa, daughter of the late Rev. Arthur Wayn, of New Town.

33.

The Mercury (Hobart, Tas. : 1860-1954) — Monday 11 October 1909 — Page 7 of 8

GOLF.

THE GROVE CLUB.

At the Grove Club links on Saturday afternoon mixed foursomes were played for handsome prizes, generously donated by Mr. Rowland Pocock, while Miss W. Pocock was the hostess for the afternoon. In addition to the prizes for the mixed foursomes, another substantial prize was offered by the same donor for clock golf, both for players and non-players. The weather was just perfect, and Miss Pocock had invited many from Hobart, who, in addition to the members, keenly enjoyed the afternoon. In the mixed foursomes the prize for ladies (a large silver photo frame) was won by Mrs. J. A. Johnson; that for the men (a pair of silver-backed brushes in case) going to J. A. Johnson. The score for this pair was, gross 104, handicap 14, net 90. The runners-up were H. Allport and Mrs. W. Campbell, with a score of 93 gross, handicap 2, net 91. The third couple up were Stewart and Miss Harrison, with 110, handicap 25, net 95. The clock golf was won by Mrs. Power, with a score of 24. The prize was a crystal and silver vase.

The Mercury (Hobart, Tas. : 1860-1954) — Tuesday 21 February 1911 — Page 2 of 8

CYCLING.

RACES AT THE GROVE.

On Saturday afternoon a couple of cycle events, the running of which was watched with considerable interest by local wheelmen, were brought off on the Grove sports ground. The results were as folols:—
Open Handicap—G. Bond, Judbury, 1; D. Talbot, Ranelagh, 2; A. Jones, Ranelagh, 3.
Maiden Race—A. Jones, Ranelagh, 1; B. Williams, Grove, 2.

34.

GOLF.

THE GROVE G.C.

The Grove Golf Club enjoyed some good foursome play for prizes donated by the captain of the club (Mr. W. J. Campbell) on Saturday.

Those starting were Mesdames W. J. Campbell, Perry Turnbull, A. Flexmore, Power, Leslie Butler, Misses Gant, Nairn, C. Cox, Paton, Messrs. Harold Wright, W. J. Campbell, Ashton Jones, J. Perry Turnbull, A. Dowling, Thorold, Power, Hull, Fell. The wind was very high at times, which rather hampered the play, but nevertheless very consistent form was shown all round. Two couples, Mrs. J. Perry Turnbull and Mr. Ashton Jones, and Miss Daphne Gant and Mr. Thorold, tied for first place, with 5: for the nine holes. When this was announced the tie was attempted to be played off, with the result that another tie was again recorded, so, as the light was waning, it was agreed to halve the prize (golf balls). The runners up were Miss Cox (Clarendon) and Mr. Arthur Dowling, who were only one stroke behind the winners, and Mrs. Flexmore and Mr. Fell were placed third, with only one stroke more. Mrs. S. E. Shoobridge provided acceptable afternoon tea, and there were many spectators of the contest, which was waged with much spirit.

This golf club, "The Grove Golf Club," are getting up a ball for the club funds on Tuesday, 23rd inst., the ladies of the club supplying the supper, and Mrs. Leslie Butler and Miss Gwen Ashton Jones supervising it. The ball is to be plain and fancy dress, and will take place in Mr. Wright's hop kiln. A late train for the convenience of town folk will leave Glenorchy at 12 (midnight). The hon. secretary is Mr. Turnbull, Bellemere, Glenorchy.

35.

FATAL ACCIDENT NEAR JERICHO.

MR. BERNARD WRIGHT FOUND DEAD.

A well-known resident of Jericho, in the person of Mr. Bernard Howard Wright, was accidentally killed yesterday.

From the meagre particulars to hand, it appears that Mr. Wright, who was manager of an estate near Jericho, was making his customary rounds on horseback when he was struck by a falling branch, and killed on the spot.

The deceased was a son of the late Mr. Stephen Wright, of the Grove, Glenorchy, and formerly manager of the Commercial Bank at St. Helens. His brothers, Messrs. Harold and Howard Wright, on receiving intimation of the accident, at once proceeded to the scene

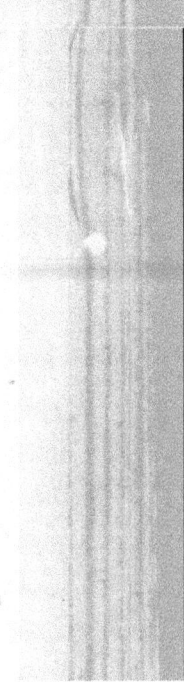

36. See "Glenorchy 1804-1964", by Alison Alexander, page 98

37.

The Mercury (Hobart, Tas. : 1860-1954), Saturday 10 May 1919, Page 6

FRUITGROWERS' ASSOCIATION

MEETING AT THE GROVE.

PROTEST AGAINST PRICE FOR BAG APPLES.

A meeting of fruitgrowers, convened by the Grove Small Fruit Association, was held at Mr. S. G. Parsons's applehouse, Grove, on Thursday night, when there was a large and representative attendance. Councillor W. Talbot presided.

Mr. David West, explaining the object of the meeting, stated that growers were only getting 1s. per bushel f.o.b. for their apples, and it was not a fair thing to continue selling at that price. What was wanted was some good system of co-operation.

Mr. Reece, Labour candidate for the Franklin division, followed, pointing out that, as that was not a political meeting, he was not there in his capacity of Labour candidate. He urged the growers present to combine with a view to getting a fair deal for their fruit.

Mr. Chas. Stubbings addressed the meeting on similar lines, as also did Mr. F. Cole.

Mr. J. J. Kenneally (manager of the Port Huon packing sheds) explained what had been done in co-operation by his association, stating that it had been selling f.o.b. Hobart at 7s. and 7s. 6d. cash before the apples were packed.

A resolution was carried to the effect that that large and representative meeting of fruitgrowers refuse to accept less than 2s. per bushel from the drying, cider, and jam factories.

A deputation, comprising several of the growers present and Mr. J. J. Kenneally, was appointed to wait upon the Premier with a view to ascertaining what assistance could be obtained towards ensuring a reasonable price for the bag apples, which it was declared were rotting on the ground. About 60 signatures were appended to a document undertaking to abide by the resolution, and not to deliver apples for less than 2s. per bushel. It is intended by the promoters of the meeting to extend their operations to the Derwent Valley, with a view to having the whole of Southern Tasmania thoroughly organised.

A further resolution was also carried agreeing to join, provisionally, all the affiliated small fruit associations being willing to do so, the Port Huon Fruitgrowers' Association Ltd., it being announced that that association was prepared to take the growers in as shareholders and establish branch sheds in their vicinity.

The Minister of Agriculture (Hon. B. Hayes), who was present at the commencement of the meeting, said that being in Launceston and hearing of the meeting, he had come along to assist the producer in any way that he could. The quarantine regulations made things very difficult just now, but the Government were determined to maintain them at all costs. He explained the steps that had been taken for the allotment of space in the South by the steamer Riverina. Applications had been received there for space for 140,000 cases of fruit. There would be no distinction between different parts of the island, and if means could be devised to get ships to come North he would help to the best of his ability. (Hear, hear.)

After a somewhat lengthy discussion, the following motions were passed:

Moved by Master Warden E. Bate, and seconded by Mr. V. Taylor,—"That the Government be asked to send Oonah or some other suitable ship to lift the perishable goods now await shipment at Launceston and the North West Coast ports."

Moved by Master Warden Bird, and seconded by Mr. Blundell,—"That a sub-committee be appointed to consider and report upon the desirability of establishing a quarantine station on the River Tamar (Middle Island), to consider whether it is possible to devise some scheme whereby shipping facilities of the port may be improved during the influenza epidemic, such as working with a double crew, as has been suggested in the South, the following to be the sub-committee:—The Mayor, President of the Chamber of Commerce, President of the Traders' Association, representative of the Marine Board, Chairman of Merchants' Association, President of the Commercial League, and Mr. V. Taylor, representing shippers."

Mr. J. J. Broomby was appointed delegate to go with Mr. Connell to Devonport on Monday next, and put the matter before the people there.

RETURNED SOLDIERS.

A WELCOME HOME.

Private Wm. B. Rankin, an Anzac, whose parents reside at 2nd Commons road, North Hobart, was welcomed home at a large function held in honour at the I.O.O.F. hall, Moir street, on Thursday evening...

38. See "Glenorchy 1804-1964", by Alison Alexander, page 178

39. Howard's death was reported in Hobart and Sydney papers, since his wife's family was from Sydney.

The Sydney Morning Herald (NSW : 1842-1954) Monday 22 September 1924 Page 8 of 16

WRIGHT.—September 6, at his residence, 92 Holebrook-place, Hobart, Howard Edward Wright, eldest son of Stephen Wright, The Grove, Glenorchy, Tasmania, aged 75 years.

Mr. Howard Edward Wright, of Holebrook Place, a well-known Hobart citizen, died at his residence on Saturday, after a severe illness. Mr. Wright had taken a prominent part in the prospecting and exploration of the West Coast in his younger days, and he was also well known as an orchardist. He was the eldest son of the late Mr. Stephen Wright, of Adelaide, and coming to Hobart with his parents at an early age, was for some time resident at "The Grove," Glenorchy. He was at one time a member of the Fisheries Board, and also took a keen interest in sport, and was connected in his youth with the New Town Football Club, while his name was not unknown in rowing circles. Of late years he had made a hobby of raising pedigree poultry. Mr. Wright married Miss Maud Rogers, a daughter of the late Judge Rogers of New South Wales, who survives him, but had no children. He was a brother of Mr. Harold Wright, of "The Grove," Glenorchy, and of Mr. Ernest Wright, while his sisters, Mrs. Winchester Bisdee and Miss Wright, also survive him. The funeral service will be held at All Saints Church to-morrow morning, commencing at 10.30 o'clock, and immediately afterwards the funeral will move to St. John's churchyard, New Town, arriving at 11.30.

Hobart Mercury Mon Sep 24 1924 p1

DEATHS.

WRIGHT.—On September 6th, at his residence, 92 Holebrook Place, Howard Edward Wright, eldest son of the late Stephen Wright, of The Grove, Glenorchy, aged 75 years.

40.

The Mercury (Hobart, Tas. : 1860-1954) Monday 25 October 1926

MOTOR-CAR OVERTURNS

OCCUPANTS ESCAPE INJURY.

A single-seater motor-car, driven by Esmond Wright, of Davey-street, Hobart, was completely upset when turning from the Main-road into Derwent Park-road on Saturday afternoon. The car, besides the driver, contained two passengers, Mr. and Mrs. James Kremmer, but beyond a few bruises, none was injured.

The car was following the progress of one of the cyclists in the road race from Ross to Hobart, and in turning the sharp corner at Derwent Park, one of the rear wheels broke in two, and the car was turned completely over, the occupants being pinned beneath. Constable Thomson and several passers-by righted the car, and the driver and his passengers picked themselves up hardly any the worse for their accident. The wind screen was shattered, but, apart from this, the car was undamaged. A spare wheel was put on in place of the one broken, and the party drove on to the T.C.A. ground to witness the finish of the cycle race.

41.

TASMANIA

The Births, Deaths and Marriages Registration Act 1999

RECORD OF DEATH

Registration No. 1690/1929

1. Surname of deceased	WRIGHT
2. Christian or other names	Maude Florence
3. Date of death	27 JULY 1929
4. Place of death	244 Davey St, HOBART
5. Occupation	Not Stated
6. Stated year of birth/age at death	68 years
7. Sex	FEMALE
8. Usual place of residence	Not Stated
9. Reputed birthplace	SYDNEY
10. Conjugal condition at death	WIDOWED
11. If ever married - Name and surname of last spouse	Howard WRIGHT
12. Issue - of all marriages	Living males / Deceased males / Living females / Deceased females
13. Age at each marriage	26 years (first) (second) (third) (etc)
14. If never married - names of parents	
15. If born overseas - Period of residency in Australia	
16. Date registered	29 JULY 1929
17. Registration officer/district	J.P. LAUGHTON

ENDORSEMENT(S)
Formerly recorded as: D H 1874 1929 F in District HOBART

Cause of Death: PHTHISIS
CARDIAC FAILURE

Medical Attendant: DR. R. WHISHAW
Informant: A J CLARK, UNDERTAKER, COLLINS ST

DEATHS.

COOPER.—On July 28, 1929, at his late residence, Ellendale, John Edward, beloved husband of Emma Cooper, in the 65th year of his age.

VINCENT.—At her brother-in-law's residence, Cygnet, on July 28, Adrienne, youngest daughter of the late George Vincent, of Hull, England. Funeral will leave the above address on Tuesday, 30th, at 2.30 p.m., for Church of England Cemetery, Cygnet.

WRIGHT.—On July 27, 1929, at her residence, No. 92 Holebrook Place, Upper Davey Street, Maude Florence, widow of the late Howard Wright, and daughter of the late Edward Rogers, Clerk of the Peace, Sydney.

42.

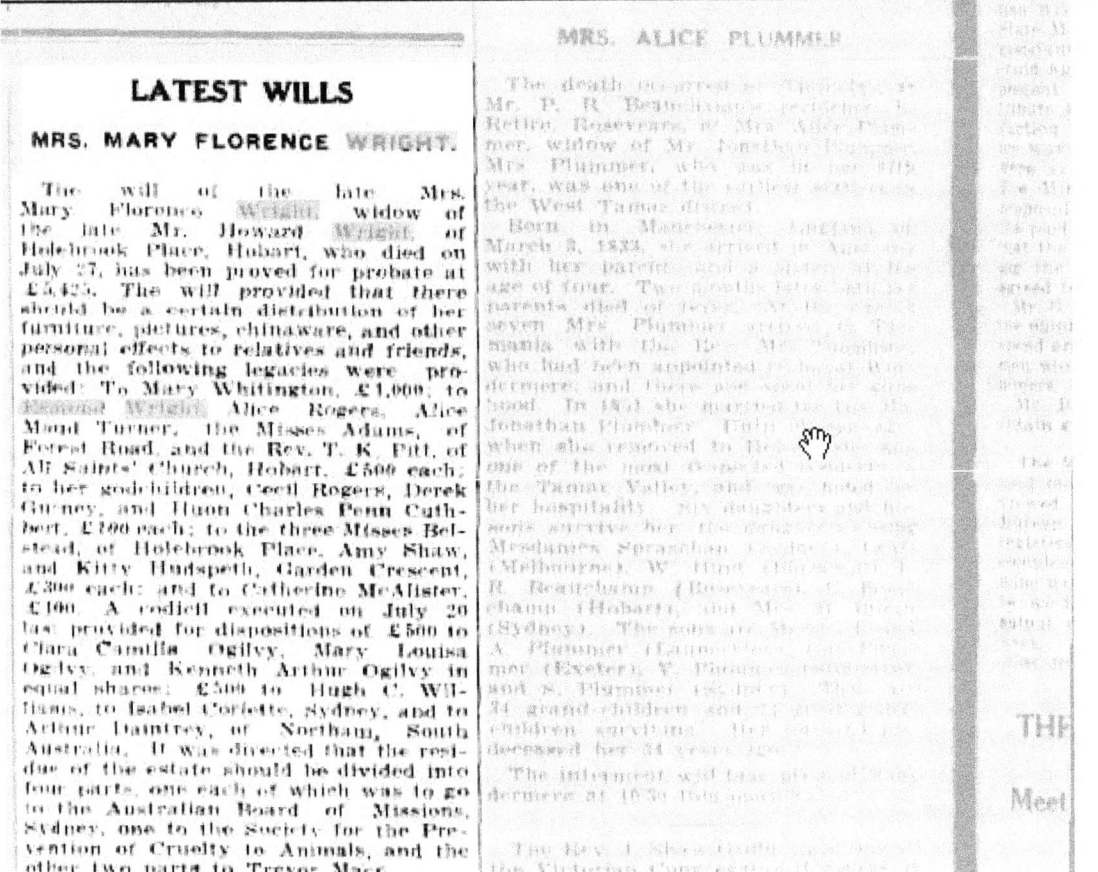

Trevor Mace was a local orchardist, living in Tolosa St., Glenorchy and active in FruitGrowers' Associations, most likely a friend of the family who may have helped Harold on the estate at times.

43.

44.

The Mercury (Hobart, Tas. : 1860-1954) — Friday 29 May 1931, Page 12 of 12

VALUABLE LIBRARY.

BURN AND SON

Are instructed by the Trustees of the Estate of the late Mrs. Howard Wright to sell by Auction, at the Rooms, Collins Street, on FRIDAY, 29th inst., at 11 o'clock sharp.

THE REMAINDER OF THE LIBRARY, about 2,000 Volumes, comprising:—
Travels, Biography, History, Belles-Lettres, Poetry, English and Foreign Classics, Standard Novels, Choicely bound Books, Etc.

45.

The Mercury (Hobart, Tas. : 1860-1954) — Saturday 17 December 1932, Page 1

DEATHS.

BAMPTON.— On December 16, 1932, at Queen Alexandra Hospital, Edward John, only son of Mr. and Mrs. E. J. Bampton, Lower Sandy Bay, aged five days.
"Suffer little children to come unto Me."

LITTLER.— Passed peacefully away at Launceston, on December 16, 1932, Helen Brand, widow of the late Frank Edwin Littler, of Everton, 2 Lyttleton Street, Launceston, loving and loved mother of Harry, Jack, and Frank, in her 71st year.

MONCUR.— Passed peacefully away at her residence, 9 Balfour Street, Launceston, on December 16, 1932, Anna Moncur, dearly beloved wife of the late William Moncur, late of Low Head, loving mother of Kate Moncur, aged 87 years.

PAUL.— On December 16, 1932, at her late residence, Alma, Bellerive, Emma, the beloved wife of H. F. Paul.

WRIGHT.— On December 16, 1932, at a private hospital, Hobart, Mary Louisa, wife of Harold Wright, The Grove, Glenorchy.

46.

The Mercury (Hobart, Tas. : 1860-1954) — Saturday 11 March 1933, Page 1 of 14

MARRIAGES.

GODLAND—WATT.— At Hobart on March 4, 1933, by special licence, Winifred Vera Watt, of Lindisfarne, Tasmania, to Gerald Godland, of Randwick, Sydney. Present address: Water-loo Street, St. Kilda, Melbourne.

WRIGHT—LONGMORE.— On March 4, 1933, at St. Michael's and All Angels' Church, by Rev. J. A. Cloudsdale, Ethel Mabel, eldest daughter of Mrs. and the late George Longmore, 6 William Street, West Hobart, to Esmond S. K., eldest son of Harold Wright, The Grove, Glenorchy.

Mr. Hugh Millar and family, of Park Street, North Hobart, wish to sincerely thank all kind friends and relatives for kindness shown, letters, telegrams, cards, and floral tributes, and personal expressions of sympathy, during their sad bereavement. Will one and all please accept this as their deepest appreciation?

The family of the late Thomas Riley, 124 Goulburn Street, wish to sincerely thank all kind friends and relatives for letters, cards, telegrams, and floral tributes received in their recent sad bereavement. Will all please accept this as a personal expression of deepest gratitude.

BIRTHS

McCOY (nee Joy Cragg).—On January 23, 1934, at St. Stephen's Hospital, to Mr. and Mrs. C. McCoy; a daughter (Joy).

WRIGHT (nee Longmore).—On January 25, 1934, at the Queen Alexandra Hospital, to the wife of Esmond Wright, 95 Montpelier Road; a son (Kennard Robert George).

---

uary 27th, 1923.
Not a day do we forget you,
In our hearts you're always near,
We who loved you sadly miss you,
As it dawns another year.
Inserted by his loving daughter, Maggie, and son-in-law, Bert, and grandsons, Bertie and Boris Vince.

JAMIESON.—In memory of Hugh Hunter Jamieson, late of Huntley Point, Sydney, died January 27, 1925. Inserted by his fond wife, Mollie Jamieson, Jericho.

LOVELESS.—In sad but loving mem—

GROVE ESPLANADE

Declared Officially Open

Ideal Reserve

In the presence of a large gathering, including Glenorchy councillors, members of Parliament, and numerous residents of Glenorchy and their children, the spacious Grove Esplanade, fronting on Elwick Bay, Glenorchy, was declared open by the Warden (Mr. R. N. J. Stourton) on Saturday. The esplanade, which has been set aside as a reserve for Glenorchy children through the efforts of the Glenorchy Council and the Grove Esplanade Improvement Committee, is ideally situated and well sheltered. Facilities for bathing have been provided, and it is the intention of the committee to plant trees in the reserve, and further to improve it.

The Warden, who was introduced by the chairman of the Improvement committee (Councillor W. J. McGann), declaring the esplanade officially open, said that it represented 12 blocks of land of the Grove estate sub-division, and comprised an area of 2¾ acres. It had been prepared at a cost of £628, and filled a want of long-standing in the municipality. He appealed to all who visited the reserve to see to it that the grounds were well kept and the trees protected from the fires of picnic parties.

Councillor T. J. Fleming spoke of the efforts of the Glenorchy Council to secure the ground as an esplanade for the people of the district.

Mr. T. Murdoch, M.L.C., and Mr. E. Brooker, M.H.A., congratulated the council on its foresight, and those responsible for raising funds and effecting the various improvements which had been made to the grounds.

The Grove Esplanade Improvement Committee comprises Councillor W. J. McGann (chairman), Messrs. H. Lane and H. Bannister (joint hon. secretaries), M. Williams (treasurer), W. L. Butterworth, T. Beakley, J. P. Kennedy, J. Fulton, E. Butterworth, E. Startup, and L. Leach.

Among those present at the opening were the Rev. F. F. Byatt, Mrs. Thomas Murdoch and Miss K. Murdoch, Mr. and Mrs. N. P. Booth, Councillor F. J. H. Hassett and Miss Hassett, Mr. and Mrs. H. Home, Mr. W. Paterson, Mr. and Mrs. P. H. Scott, Mrs. Samuel Smith, Miss Brewer, Councillor J. Craig, Messrs. J. H. Geappen, H. H. Batten, W. Neilson (Collinsvale), and Harold Wright.

Afternoon tea was provided by a committee of Glenorchy women.

GOLDEN WEDDING

CELEBRATION AT HOBART.

MR. AND MRS. JOHN CARRIER.

Mr. and Mrs. John Carrier, of Long Beach, Lower Sandy Bay, celebrated their golden wedding yesterday, the marriage having been celebrated at St. David's Cathedral, Hobart, on February 10, 1885, by the Rev. J. Gray.

MR. AND MRS. JOHN CARRIER, Of Hobart, who celebrated their golden wedding anniversary yesterday.

Numerous letters of congratulation were received, and among those who called to offer their felicitations were some of the guests at the wedding breakfast.

Mr. and Mrs. Carrier have had a family of 14 children, 10 of whom are living. Nine are married, and there are 30 grandchildren. Before being married Mr. Carrier made several whaling trips. Later he worked as a winchman on the wharf for over 30 years. For the last 20 years he has carried on business at Long Beach.

Mr. and Mrs. Carrier and friends tonight will be the guests of their family at an evening at the Continental.

PUBLIC WORKS DEPARTMENT

TENDERS ACCEPTED.

The following tenders have been accepted by the Department of Public Works:—Gladstone police quarters, erection, H. D. French, Bridport, £678 10s.; University of Tasmania, additions to biological building, J. Andrewartha, Hobart, £1,289; Roland State school and residence, repairs and painting, J. W. Sellars, Sheffield, £130 10s.; Staverton State school and residence, repairs and painting, H. G. Haslock, Devonport, £133; Gormanston State school, fencing, C. V. Boote, Queenstown, £63 14s.; Don State school residence, repairs and painting, H. G. Haslock, Devonport, £78 12s. 6d.; Somerset State school and residence, repairs and painting, W. Lee Burnie, £106; Lightho

49.

The Mercury (Hobart, Tas. : 1860-1954), Tuesday 13 August 1940, Page 6 of 8

FORTHCOMING SALES

CLEARING SALE FURNITURE, IMPLEMENTS, etc., a/c H. S. R. Wright, The Grove, Glenorchy, Wednesday, August 14.

50.

The Mercury (Hobart, Tas. : 1860-1954), Monday 5 January 1942, Page 5 of 6

Mr. Harold S. R. Wright

Mr. Harold S. R. Wright, a prominent resident of the Glenorchy municipality for many years, died in a private hospital at Hobart yesterday in his 91st year.

Mr. Wright left England with his parents in 1854. They settled in Adelaide, where Mr. Wright's father was Mayor of Glenelg. Mr. Wright came to Tasmania about 1866 and settled at Glenorchy. In his younger days he was an all-round athlete, a good rower, sculler and footballer. He was an authority on the earlier days of Hobart, and was Warden of Glenorchy for many years. He was associated with those responsible for the introduction of a water supply scheme for the district. He took a keen interest in district affairs, and interested himself in church work, and was a member of St. Paul's Church of England, Glenorchy. He was a big landholder in Glenorchy, and owned The Grove estate.

Mr. Wright is survived by a son, Mr. Esmond Wright, Sandy Bay, and a daughter, Miss K. I. H. Wright, Fern Tree. His wife died about 50 years ago.

The cremation will take place at Cornelian Bay tomorrow.

51.

The Mercury (Hobart, Tas. : 1860-1954), Wednesday 5 January 1949, Page 6 of 12

husband of Hilda Smithies, of 355 Huon Rd. No flowers, by request.

WRIGHT—On January 4, 1949, at a private hospital, Hobart, Kate, only daughter of the late Harold and Kate Wright, of the Grove, Glenorchy.

FUNERAL NOTICES

GLASSHOUSES, IMPLEMENTS, ETC.
at
"The Grove," Glenorchy

Under instruction from Mr. B. Mollineaux we will hold a Clearing Sale of Implements and sundries at "The Grove," Wrights Avenue, Glenorchy, on February 1, at 1 o'clock:

12 h.p. Howard Rotary Hoe and loading Planks; 6 h.p. Howard Rotary Hoe; 3 h.p. Cultivator (incomplete); 1928 Chevrolet Utility; 1937 3-ton Dodge lorry (wrecked); 6 h.p. Moffat Petrol-Kero Engine; Steel Cabinet, Motors, Saw Bench with two saws and 3in. Rubber Belting; 6 h.p. Underfired Boiler — 100lb. pressure — Govt. Certificate; Sliding Docker Saw; 3/8 h.p. single phase Motor; 3 h.p Vertical Tube Boiler; Minton Seed Sower; Wheel Hoe; Rega Duster; 2 spray Pumps; Hand concrete mixer; 2 wheel barrows — one rubber tyred; 2 clock face scales; Portable forge; Overland Lorry, 4 engine; Walnut logs; Spouting and Down Pipe, in suitable lots; 500ft. 1in. pipe; 4,200ft. ¾in. pipe; ½in. pipe; 4,000 Plant trays, various sizes in suitable lots; Flower Pots; Horticultural Glass; Coil Barb Wire; Plain Wire; Wire Netting, Bean Sticks; 44-gal. drum; Petrol Pump; 15 60ft. Hoses; Galv. Iron; Galv. Cover strips; 2 Grindstones; Timber; 250ft. V. Jointed Hardwood; Extension Ladder; Trestles and Planks; Nails; Pipe fittings; Hot water taps; Steam and Water stop Valves; Flower and Vegetable Seeds; Pipe Stocks and Dies, ½in. to 1¼in.; Pipe Cutters and Vice; Hand Truck; Tools, 5-ton Stump Jack; Paint; Garden Tiles; Diabolo Separator; Bagley Vice; 2 Chimney Cowls; Sundries; Pot Plants; Seedlings; Polyanthus Crowns for removal by March 1, 1952.

Glass House 48ft. x 12ft., with 6 1¼in. Steam Coils; Glass House 57 x 12; 48 x 12 Glass House; 51 x 15ft. Glass House; 3 4ft. x 12ft. Frames; 7 30ft. x 4ft. Frames; 1 50ft. x 4ft. Frame; 75 x 12 Bush House; 51 x 12ft. Bush House; 6 Compost Bins and 24 cubic yds. Compost.

Surplus Furniture includes: Kitchen chairs; Kitchen cabinet; round table; small tables; lino, mats; mantel radio; Fowlers jars, some full; Ladies' Austral Bicycle; Moffat Electric Stove; Kitchen sundries.

On Account of Other Owner—

Also small Speed Boat — unfinished; small Metal Turning Lathe with 3 chucks; 400ft. Galv. Corr. Iron; 3 High Trestles; 10ft. Dinghy; 50ft. 3/8 Galv. Chain; 3 lengths 16in. Ridge Capping.

A. G. WEBSTER & SONS LTD.

Chapter 3

1. http://www.cmhpf.org/kids/Guideboox/brick.html

Vocabulary

COURSE - a row of bricks.

HEADER - short side of the brick faces out.

STRETCHER - long side of the brick faces out.

Flemish Bond

This pattern is made from alternating **headers** and **stretchers** on each course.

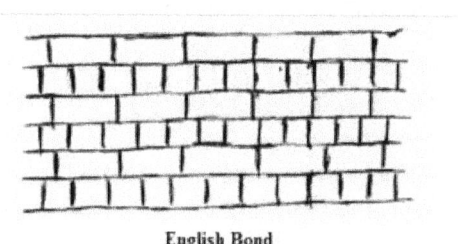

English Bond

This pattern is made from alternating **courses** of headers with courses of stretchers.

2.

The Mercury (Hobart, Tas. : 1860-1954) about ◀ Monday 29 July 1929 ▶ ◀ Page 8 ▼ of 14 ▶

PERSONAL

OBITUARY.

Mrs. Howard Wright.

Mrs. Howard Wright died at her residence, Holebrook Place, on Saturday. Her most outstanding characteristic was her warm-hearted sympathy with anyone in trouble. Her generosity is remembered by many people now living in other States and distant lands during the war. She was greatly esteemed by soldiers in camps and hospitals, which she visited regularly, and later, when hostilities ceased, she continued to work unceasingly for the Diggers, many of whom found the "battle of life" more terrible than any experience of the war. Mrs. Wright's home in Holebrook Place, with its spacious grounds, was very often a convalescent home for soldiers just out of hospital. Having travelled very extensively, and being conversant with the best literature of her own and continental countries, she always was a most interesting conversationalist. The funeral takes place in St. John's Cemetery, New Town, this morning, and is to be preceded by a service in All Saints' Church at 9.30 a.m.

3. Lilian Overell was a world traveller, women's supporter and outspoken local citizen. Newspaper clippings representative of her doings and interest are shown below.

NEW GUINEA. —

MISS LILIAN OVERELL'S EXPERIENCES.

Many interesting experiences were related last night at the Memorial-hall, Hobart, by Miss Lilian Overell, sister of Miss Louise Overell, the latter lady being secretary of the Tasmanian branch of the Soudan Mission. The occasion was a lantern lecture given by Miss Overell on her impressions of New Guinea territory, on behalf of the funds of the mission. Miss Overell has resided for an extended period in the territory, on which she lectured on ably, a good deal of the time she spent there having been passed in the island of New Britain.

The Mayor (Alderman J. Soundy) presided, and he expressed his regret that the attendance was not so large as could have been wished in view of the object for which the lecture was being given, the Soudan Mission doing such good work. He referred to the lecturer as the authoress of, a book entitled "A Woman's Impressions of German New Guinea," and spoke of her extreme knowledge of that country.

Miss Overell first explained the geographical features of the islands which her lecture concerned, and by means of about 64 lantern slides was able to illus-

The Mercury Wed 24 Sep 1924 p4 of 12

MUSSOLINI IN A STORM.

PERTH, Thursday.

Miss Lilian Overell, Tasmanian delegate to the quinquennial congress of the International Council of Women held at Vienna in May and June, passed through Fremantle on the Moreton Bay to-day. She said that many women, especially Germans, thought that the League of Nations had not accomplished as much as it should for world peace.

While Miss Overell was in Rome a great storm caused 60,000 people at a sports meeting to flee for shelter, but Mussolini stood bareheaded with folded arms in the centre of the area as though defying the elements.

SMH Fri Oct 3 1930 p 10 of 18

FRANKLIN SQUARE

To the Editor of "The Mercury."

I wish to support Mr. Oldham's protest against any part of Franklin Square being filched away, no matter for how good a purpose.

The little-used children's reserve behind the Town Hall is the obvious place for the child welfare building.

Franklin Square is a beautiful spot, and "a thing of beauty" should be "a joy for ever." This delightful reserve, with its fresh greenery against the background of fine public buildings, and its rare historic interest, is of unique value increased still more by its statue with the inscription ---

"Not here; The cold North hath thy bones,

But thou, heroic sailor soul,

Art passing on thy happier voyage now.

Towards no earthly goal."

I sincerely hope such an unfortunate mistake will be rectified while it is still in its initial stages.

LILIAN OVERELL.

A NEEDED BUS SERVICE.

Residents in the neighbourhood of Holebrook Place, the Huon Road, and the Waterworks Road have petitioned for many years for a system of transport. The idea of continuing the tramlines up Wentworth or Darcy Streets will not prove satisfactory, for what is needed is a motor or trolley omnibus service from near the Town Hall to Congress Street. This will meet the needs of all residents, and will prevent the excessive overcrowding on the Cascades trams. As many as 75 passengers have been carried by the little one-man trams! Is this safe or sanitary? Cannot the health officers see that the overcrowding of our badly-ventilated trams is a menace to the community, especially during epidemics? Houses recently sold in this locality realised only about half their value. This means a loss in city rates. A better method of transport would soon increase the ratable property, and balance any initial loss on the omnibus service.

LILIAN OVERELL.

The Mercury Wed 8 May 1929 p 2 of 12

The Mercury Sat 27 Apr 1929 p7 of 16

4.

5. Evidence of the interchangeability of Upper Davey St and Holebrook Place

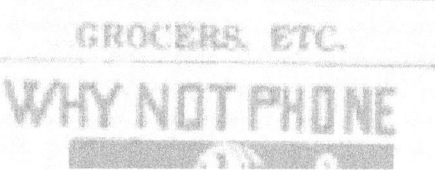

Under instructions from the owner—
OUTSTANDING FAMILY HOME
MONTANA 298 DAVEY ST, HOLEBROOK PLACE.
VACANT POSSESSION.

ALL THAT gentleman's superior residence and grounds

6.

Holebrook place
Right hand side from Davey st
Barclay Mrs Margt
Heyer Rev J (Pres)
.......here is Weld st..........
Gunn F Lindsay (Crisp & Co, Ld)
Ward Mrs Moses, brdg house
Pringle E Neville, "Hillcrest"
.......here is Anglesea st........
McGuffie Richd
Turner Ernest W, pol mag
Escott Wm H

HOBART DIRECTORY.
Strutt Misses
Dawson Chas B
Ellis J C
..........here is Darcy st..........
Walter Chas E
Crozier Leslie J
......here is City boundary......
Morris Ernest A, Glenbrook
......here is Wentworth st......
Left hand side from Davey st
Reid Mrs L M, Rathobank
Hall Robt
Ellis John C, Lebrena
Chapman Geoffrey V
Chapman J Robison
Fitzgerald Thos, Bendena
Peacock Ernest A, jp (H Jones & Co, Ld), Cambooree
Patterson Mrs B C, Varuna
Simmons Matthw W (Wolfhagen, S & Walch)
Wahroonga Girls' School (Miss L Overell)
Wright Howard E
Smith Miss M C
Cobbett Profr Pitt
.......Reform st, City bndry.......
White Robt T, Moretta
White Horace B
Wright Ernst C
Daniels Hy J
Rivers R Godfrey
De Houghton Thos
......Huon rd & Romilly st......

Postal Directory 1919 Page_102 Holebrook Place Wright Howard E, also Wright Ernst C. See
http://catalogue.statelibrary.tas.gov.au/item/?id=981598

```
.... Here is Elboden st ....
216 Reid Mrs Lucy M
220 Massey Mrs M J
Ellis John C, "Lebrena"
Chapman Geoffrey V
Chapman James R
Fitzgerald Thos, "Bendena"
234 Peacock Ernest A, JP
236 Patterson Mrs Elsie C
Hall Thos, "Varuna"
238 Simmons Matthw W
240 Overell Miss Lillian
244 Wright Albert C
254 Smith Misses M E, M C,
    & G D
256 Shadforth P Stephen
........ Reform st ........
260 White Robt T
262 White Horace B
264 Wright Ernest C
266 Daniels Hy J
268 Rivers Richd G
270 De Hoghton Mrs Julia
... Romilly st & Huon rd ..
```

```
TASMANIA TOWNS DIRECTORY.

For continuation see Sandy
    Bay rd)

Hill st
Right side from Melville st
  Fennell Wm
  Cracknell Mrs Jessie
  Howard Mrs Susan
  .. Here is Brisbane st ...
  Marquis of Hastings htl
    (Jas Parkinson)
  Maher Wm
1 Maher Miss Tessie
3 Powell Ed L
5 Chatterton Jos W
7 Williams Mrs Elizbth
7 Williams Miss G, tchr mus
```

```
. Here is Lansdowne cres .
110 Boon Edwin
112 Issell Louis
114 Howard Wm W
116 Hawson Eric
118 Underwood Jesse
.. Hamilton st intersects ..
120 Mason Edwd
124 Barren Wallace
128 Batchelor Jno A
130 Sweet Tasman
132 Oliver Robt
134 Proctor Richd O
.... Here is Arthur st ....
Holebrook Pl, see continua-
    tion Davey st
```

LEFT - Postal Directory 1921 Page_51 244 Davey St Wright Albert (should be Howard) C, also Ernest C at 264

and

RIGHT - Postal Directory 1921 Page_62 Holebrook place - see continuation Davey St.

7.

```
.... Here is Elboden st ....
220 Newman Geo
224 Vacant
226 Corney E Whitaker
228 Sampson Theo
Fitzgerald Thos, "Bendena"
234 Giblin Thos, med pract
236 Bloomfield D F
236 Hinchliffe G L
236 Harrison Derek
236 Wood Austin
236 Brinton Irwin
236 Player J H
236a Taylor Prof A B
238 Townley Mrs Har
240 Overell Miss Lillian
244 Monfries Jno E
244 Murray Jos B
244 Featherstone M
252 Lewis A N
254 Mitchell Mrs Thos
256 Morgan L G
256 Law W Bruce
256 Mather Andw
256a Hungerford Mrs L
    Hathaway House
258 Andrew Wm J
    Lynton av ......
260 White Robt T
262 Hutchin Arth W
264 Robertson Wm
266 Grant Chas W
268 Rivers Mrs G
270 Onslow G Fras
272 Moore Clif R
.. Romilly st & Huon rd ..
    David av Sandy Bay
```

```
....... Elboden st ........
286 Newman Geo
288 Baker Mrs Ada
288 Brown Frnk T
294 Bloomfield Percy W*
294 Eaves Geo
294 Hull L Norm
294 Miller Mrs Frances
294 Bryan C Jno
296 Chambers Herbt G
298 Sampson Theo
300 Fitzgerald Thos*
300 Hawker C R
308 Cunningham A B, med
    pract
314 Bloomfield Derek F*
314 Carrick Miss E E
314 Brinton Irwin
314 Brown O L
314 Hinchliffe G L
314 Lewis Jno
316 Taylor Prof A B*
320 Aust Women's Army Serv
    (barracks)
326 Overell Miss Lillian*
328 Monfries Jno E*
328 Marsden Mrs Ilma
332 Rex Guy
334 Mitchell Mrs Josephine*
336 Mather Andw*
340 Edgell Bayard H
342 Richardson Robt E*
........ Lynton av ........
344 White Mrs Robt T
346 Hutchin Arth W*
348 Robertson Wm*
350 Clark Mrs H Inglis
350 Van de Ven C W
350 Kalbfell Robt J
352 Rivers Mrs G*
354 Onslow G Fras
    ........ Romilly st ........
    ........ Huon rd ........
```

LEFT - Postal Directory 1939 Page_20   244 Davey St - Monfries Jno E and Murray and Featherstone. Lillian Overell still next door at 240

RIGHT - Postal Directory 1945 Page_21 328 Davey St - Monfries Jno E and Marsden Mrs Ilma. Lillian Overell still next door at 326

8. Sir William Dobson's home called 'Holebrook House'. Photo between 1870 and 1890

The house actually faced Lynton Ave

9. The 1947 relevant drainage plan is shown here in part as is the relevant area Google area satellite picture.

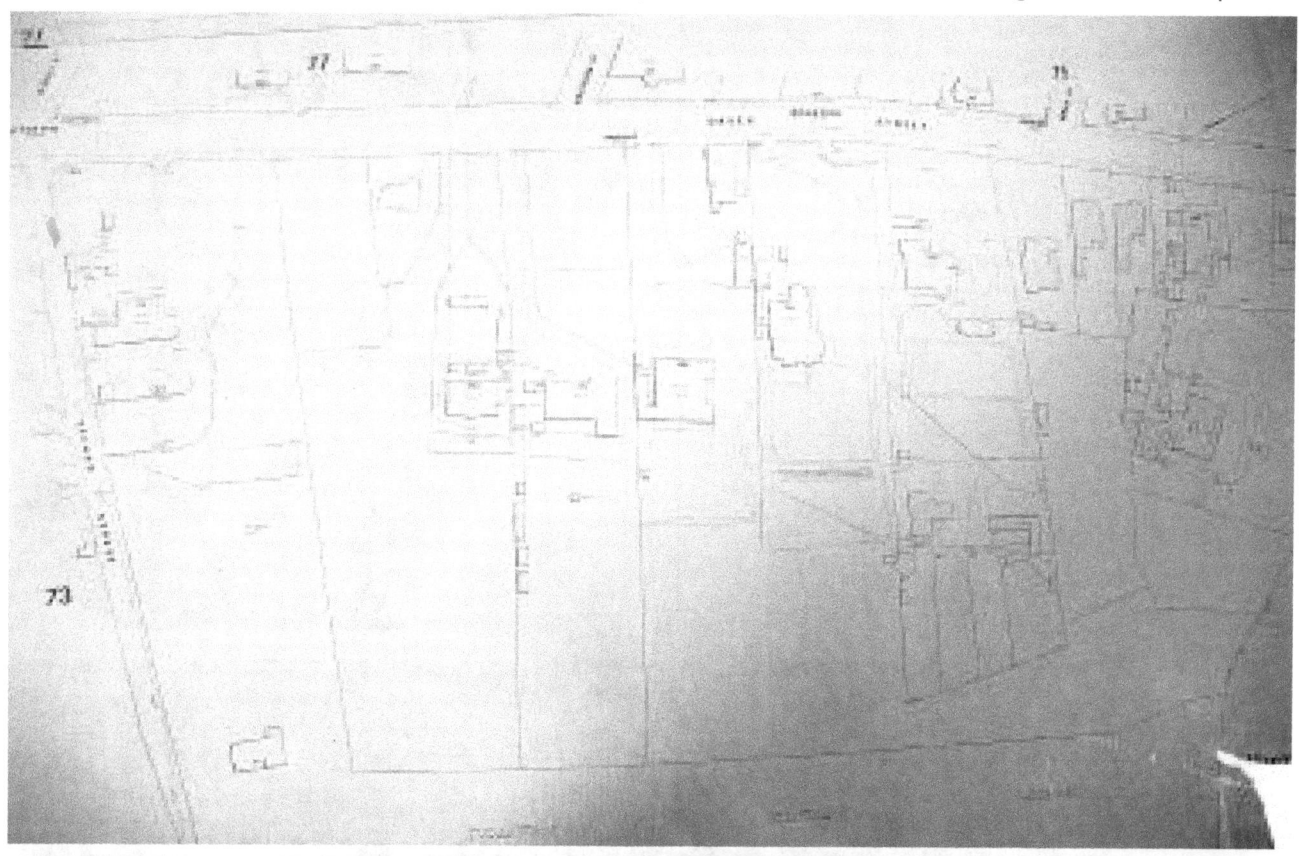

Common points in the two images are revealed below

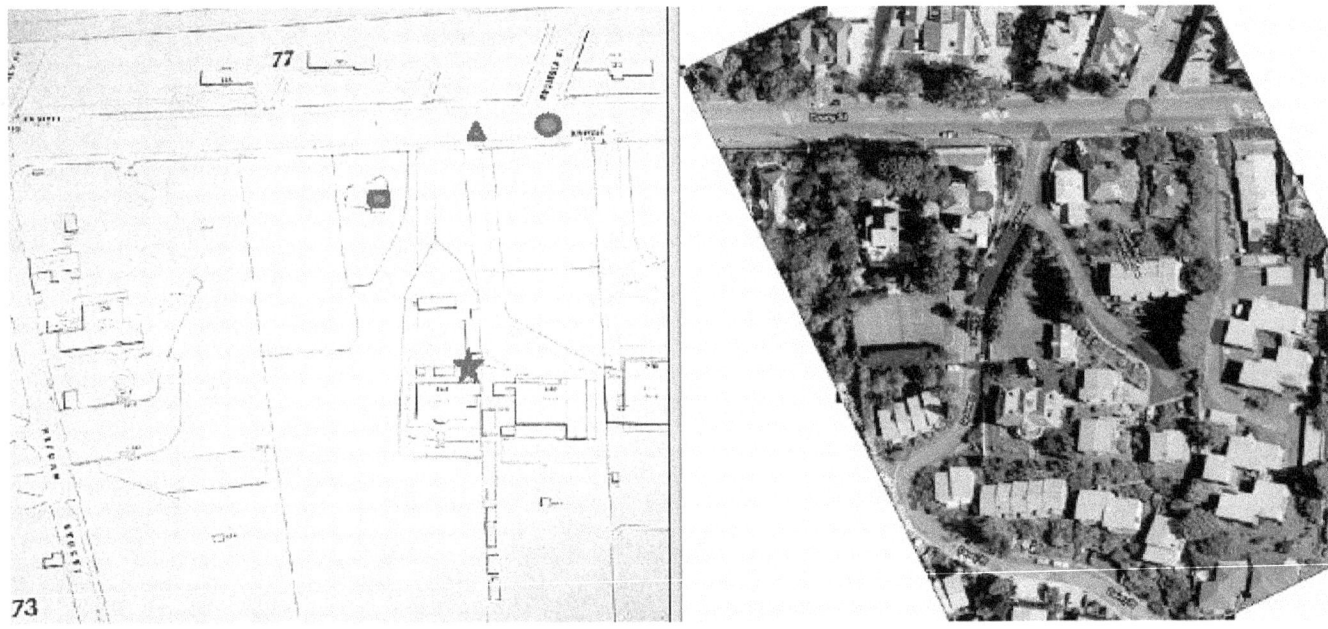

Upper Davey St.

Elboden St. to Lynton Ave was once known as Holebrook Place.

10. Much of this history has been provided by Ms. Gwenda Sheridan in personal communication. She met with Kenneth von Bibra who provided the coachmen information and other historical data about the estate.

11. Again reference is due to Ms. Gwenda Sheridan's conversations with Lady Ferrall in July 2010

12. There are 3 pages to Maude's will and codicil reproduced below

---

9³

Duty paid hereon - £574/18/2 - 5/12/29

In the Supreme Court of Tasmania.
(ECCLESIASTICAL JURISDICTION.)

17565

Gross value sworn under £ 5425

Be it Known that MAUDE FLORENCE WRIGHT late of Hobart in Tasmania Widow deceased

died on the twenty seventh **day of** July 1929 **at** Hobart aforesaid

And be it further Known that at the date hereunder written the last Will and Codicil of the said deceased was proved in the Supreme Court of Tasmania, and that administration of all the estate which by law devolves to and vests in the personal representatives of the said deceased was granted by the aforesaid Court to CHARLES D'ARCY CUTHBERT of Hobart aforesaid Solicitor one of the Executors named in the said Will TREVOR ELLIS MACE (in the Will called "Trevor Mace") of Hobart aforesaid Civil Engineer having by writing under his hand dated the eighth day of October 1929 renounced Probate thereof

Dated this ninth **day of** December 1929

MURDOCH CUTHBERT & CLARKE
Proctors Hobart

A. G. BRAMHALL

Registrar.

18 fols. THIS IS THE LAST WILL of me MAUDE FLORENCE WRIGHT of Holebrook Place Hobart in Tasmania Widow Whereof I APPOINT CHARLES D'ARCY CUTHBERT and TREVOR MACE both of Hobart aforesaid Executors and Trustees I GIVE AND BEQUEATH the following legacies namely (1) Such of my late husband Howard's silver as is in the servants room at my house in Holebrook Place Hobart by my said husband's special request and express wish to Henry Howard of Blenheim New Zealand (2) My small tea pot in the same room to Alice Bowring who was for many years in my service (3) Three boxes in the attics of my said house and my grand-father's camphor trunk with contents except my Paisley shawl to Madge Overell (4) My Paisley shawl to my niece Alice Rogers (5) All my lace to the said Alice Rogers and Lilian Overell share and share alike (6) My diamond ring and three little tables in the drawing room to my said house to the said Lilian Overell (7) My hall dresser to Florie Owens of Malvern Victoria (the transport expenses of which shall be paid for out of my residuary estate) (8) My curios and pictures to Louisa Overell (9) Three pieces of my best china to be selected by her to Rosalie Shaw of Swansea Tasmania (10) All my books to the Ladies College Sydney (11) My three little lacquer tables to Lilian Overell (12) To Mary Whitington one thousand pounds (13) To Edmond Wright Five hundred pounds (14) To the

said Alice Rogers Five hundred pounds (15) To Alice Maud Turner Five hundred pounds (16) To the four Misses Adams of No. 41 Forest Road Hobart Five hundred pounds equally between them (17) To Winifred Overell Ten pounds (18) To Louisa Overell One hundred pounds (19) To my god-children Cecil Rogers, Derek Gurney and Huon Charles Penn-Cuthbert One hundred pounds each (20) To Reverend T. K. Pitt of "All Saints" Rectory Hobart Five hundred pounds (21) To Amy Shaw of Anglesea Street Hobart Three hundred pounds (22) To the three Misses Belstead of Holebrook Place Hobart Three hundred pounds equally between them (23) To Kitty Hudspeth of Garden Crescent Hobart Three hundred pounds and (24) To Catherine McAlister one hundred pounds And I direct that all the above legacies shall be free of Probate or Estate Duties which shall be paid out of my residuary estate I GIVE DEVISE AND BEQUEATH the rest of my personal property (inclusive of any funds over which I may have a power of appointment) and all my real property to my said Trustees UPON TRUST to sell and convert the same into money and after payment thereout of the above legacies or so much thereof as my ready moneys shall not be sufficient to pay and of my debts funeral and testamentary expenses inclusive of all Probate and Estate Duties to divide the said trust moneys into four equal parts and to pay one fourth part to the Australian Board of Missions Sydney for the advancement of the objects thereof (the receipt of the Treasurer thereof to be a good discharge to my Executors) Another fourth part to the Society for the Prevention of Cruelty to Animals for the advancement of the objects thereof (the receipt of the Treasurer thereof to be a good discharge to my Executors) and the remaining two fourth parts shall be paid to the said Trevor Mace for his own use and benefit AND I DIRECT that my Trustees may in the realisation of my estate at once sell by private treaty to Mr. A. E. Lewis or his nominee by private contract up to approximately ninety feet of the street frontage of my land at Holebrook Place with a depth of about one hundred and thirty feet at the price of Eleven pounds per foot reserving if they deem it advisable in pursuance of any sub-divisional scheme of the balance of the said land about twenty feet for the widening through out of the Avenue leading to the Syndal Smith's property and that the balance of the said land may be sub-divided into building allotments if my Trustees think fit and so disposed of with power for my Trustees to construct such street or streets as shall be deemed advisable by them for the purposes of such sub-division and to charge the balance of the said land or any moneys payable for land sold with the cost of such construction and to postpone the sale of that part of my estate for the carrying out of any such scheme of subdivision And I further direct that any Executor or Trustee of this my Will being a Solicitor and practicing as such shall be entitled to charge and be paid all ordinary professional costs and fees for any work done or services rendered by him or his firm in the proof of this my Will and in the general administration of the trusts and directions thereof and in the realisation and winding up of my estate IN WITNESS WHEREOF I have hereunto set my hand this eighteenth day of July One thousand nine hundred and twenty nine - - - - - - - - - -

- - - - - - - .   M. F. WRIGHT   - - - - - - -

SIGNED by the above named Testatrix in the presence of us both being present at the -

same time time who in her presence and in the presence of each other have hereunto subscribed our names as witnesses RALPH WHISHAW 159 Macquarie St. Hobart R. M. CLARKE Solicitor Hobart - - - - -

THIS IS A CODICIL to the last Will of me MAUDE FLORENCE WRIGHT of Hobart in Tasmania - Widow I GIVE AND BEQUEATH the following further legacies:- (1) To Clara Camilla Ogilvy Mary Louisa Ogilvy and Kenneth Arthur Ogilvy Five hundred pounds equally between them (2) To Isabel Corlette of Sydney Five hundred pounds (3) To Hugh Williams of Hobart Sharebroker Five hundred pounds and (4) To Arthur Daintrey of Northam South Australia Five hundred pounds AND I DIRECT that in the realisation of my estate my Trustees shall in their absolute and uncontrolled discretion have power to postpone the sale of the whole or any part of my lands for such time or times as they shall think fit without being liable for any consequential loss and my Trustees shall have power to sell my lands or any part or parts thereof by public auction or private contract at such prices and on such terms as they shall think proper and to accept purchase money by instalments under contracts of sale at such rates of interest as they think fit AND I FURTHER DIRECT that in the event of my ready moneys not being sufficient to fully pay all monetary legacies bequeathed by me then such legacies or so much thereof as may be unpaid shall await the sale and realisation of my lands (subject to the above directions) and the legatees shall not be entitled to claim interest on the amount of any unpaid legacies And in all other respects I hereby confirm the contents of my said Will IN WITNESS WHEREOF I have hereunto set my hand this twentieth day of July One thousand nine hundred and twenty nine - - - -

- - - - - -   M. F. WRIGHT   - - - - - -

SIGNED by the Testatrix the said Maude Florence Wright as and for a Codicil to her last Will in the presence of us both being present at the same time who at her request in her sight and presence and in the sight and presence of each other have hereunto subscribed our names as witnesses C. D'ARCY CUTHBERT Solicitor Hobart R. M. CLARKE Solr Hobart --

13. http://www.rba.gov.au/calculator/annualPreDecimal.html

Thank you for buying this book.

For a CD containing a colour version of this entire volume

in pdf format please contact the author at

aussiewd@live.com

stating your name and address.

We'll be happy to send you further information.